EVERYBODY NEEDS TRAINING

Proven Success Secrets for the
Professional Fitness Trainer
—How to Get More Clients,
Make More Money, Change More Lives

By Danny Kavadlo

EVERYBODY NEEDS TRAINING

By Danny Kavadlo

Published in the United States by: Dragon Door Publications, Inc.
5 East County Rd B, #3 • Little Canada, MN 55117
Tel: (651) 487-2180 • Fax: (651) 487-3954
Credit card orders: 1-800-899-5111 • Email: support@dragondoor.com • Website: www.dragondoor.com

ISBN 10: 0-938045-73-3   ISBN 13: 978-0-938045-73-1

This edition first published in December, 2013
Printed in China

BOOK DESIGN AND COVER: Derek Brigham, site: www.dbrigham.com • (763) 208-3069 • Email: bigd@dbrigham.com

PHOTOGRAPHY: Jordan Perlson, Al Kavadlo, Danny Kavadlo, Jennifer Regan-Kavadlo, Matt Mendelsohn, Audra May Photography, Wes Sanchez, Magnus Unnar, Giovanni Reda & Christina Cipriano

FEATURED TATTOOS
Mask Tattoos by Louis Andrew • Buddha Belly by Benny • Backpiece by Louis Andrew

MODELS: Beth Andrews, Jasmine Brooks, Frederick Drejfald, Meng He, Kelly Jo Johnson, Al Kavadlo, Rachel Kuhns, Janelle LaCoille, Bryan Longchamp, Billy Marti, Errick McAdams, Jeff Monfleury, Jose Mota, Jennifer Noland, Lincoln Oliver, Jordan Perlson, Drew Pesale, Allegra Poggio, Jason Quick, Rick Richards, Raul Robinson, Joe Ronzo, Maria Simone, Lauren Sison, Nathaniel Smith Jr, Maria Tapia, Parichart Thepvongs & Marvin Ward

DISCLAIMER: The author and publisher of this material are not responsible in any manner whatsoever for any injury that may occur through following the instructions contained in this material. The activities, physical and otherwise, described herein for informational purposes only, may be too strenuous or dangerous for some people and the reader(s) should consult a physician before engaging in them.

"I AM A GREAT BELIEVER IN LUCK.
THE HARDER I WORK, THE MORE LUCK I HAVE."
—COLEMAN COX

TABLE OF CONTENTS

FOREWORD

Why Everybody Needs "Everybody Needs Training"

By Al Kavadlo

Throughout my childhood, my brother Danny was one of my biggest inspirations. When I look back, it's easy to see Danny's influence in a lot of my early choices. Danny listened to heavy metal, so I listened to heavy metal. Danny played the drums, so I played the drums. Danny got a tattoo, so I had to get some ink, too! Danny even got into working out before I did. After all, I was the little brother - it was natural for me to emulate a lot of what my big brother did.

People are often surprised to hear that Danny's older than me. Between his youthful exuberance and that thick head of hair, many assume he's younger. When Danny and I were kids, however, there was far less confusion. The half-decade age gap between us was a lot more significant back then. After all, when you're only five years old, a ten year-old is double your age! Now that we're both in our thirties, the disparity seems to matter a lot less.

Growing up, Danny helped me learn a lot about life, relationships, and the world at large. Though I followed in his footsteps during my formative years, I was the one who started in the fitness industry first. In adulthood, I helped convince Danny to change careers and become a personal trainer. It was cool for me to be the one who inspired him this time - I was excited to return the favor. Funny thing is, a lot of the life lessons I learned from Danny early on helped me be a better personal trainer. This is part of why I knew he would be so good at it!

When Danny began working at the gym where I had already been employed for some time, suddenly our co-workers knew him as "Al's Brother." After spending my teenage years being known as "Danny's Brother" to everyone in the neighborhood, having the roles reversed felt very strange.

Yet just like our age disparity didn't matter once we were both adults, it didn't take long for Danny to catch up as a trainer and establish an identity in the fitness industry that was all his own. In fact, Danny built his personal training career faster than just about anyone else I've ever met. He went from being brand new to the business to becoming one of the busiest trainers in one of NYC's top facilities in less than one year.

Danny is the type of guy that will succeed at whatever he puts his mind to. He's stubborn in the best possible way and he has a better work ethic than 99% of people I've ever met in my life. Whether it means waking up at the crack of dawn or working til the wee hours of the night, Danny is willing to do whatever it takes to get the job done. Once he decided to pursue an opening in fitness management, he went on to make a huge reputation for himself in that field as well. It wasn't long before people in the industry got to know the name Danny Kavadlo for his personal accomplishments and expertise. Being my brother was irrelevant.

With writing professionally, I again got started a few years before Danny and encouraged him to pursue the same path after having had some success myself. Just like I knew Danny would make a fine personal trainer, I recognized he could achieve big things in the realm of fitness writing. I had complete confidence that Danny was capable of creating a great book like this one and I'm proud to have helped give him the push to do so. After having now read the book, it's even better than I thought it would be. Danny's anecdotes and advices are entertaining, informative and insightful. Yet even more than that, his honesty is bold and refreshing.

Though much of what you'll read here might seem like common sense, other things may surprise or even shock you; some people may not be ready for all of the cold, hard truth about the personal training industry that you'll find in these pages. *Everybody Needs Training* is the real deal on the fitness business directly from someone who's done it all. It's a must-read for any serious-minded personal trainer.

Danny has laid out a stellar blueprint for fitness industry superstardom; implementing his advice is sure to take your training career to the next level. Of course, as Danny will tell you, it's not going to come easy - you're going to have to hustle! If fitness is what you live and breathe, however, everything you need to do to make your dream job a reality is in these pages. Just remember to keep an open mind - it might not be what you expect.

Al Kavadlo

FOREWORD

Danny Kavadlo and the Gonzo Brotherhood

By Marty Gallagher,
author of *The Purposeful Primitive*,
3-time World Masters Powerlifting Champion

worked for Muscle & Fitness magazine at the height of the magazine era. We were King Kong in the fitness trade world; M&F had a half-million monthly subscribers, another couple million in newsstand and overseas sales – Dr. Jim Wright, the longtime science editor for Flex mag, brought me onboard. I had 90 + feature articles published – including five in one issue; I sat front row center at the Olympia and Arnold and my niche was training – I quizzed the living hell out of the best in the world about how they trained (lifting and cardio) and how they ate. Everyone else, the staff guys, dreaded being assigned to do training articles – I loved it. The guys I interviewed got that I was really in the deal (IPF world master champion powerlifter with an 800 squat) and they opened up to me and we made training article music together...

Perhaps the most intelligent bodybuilder I ever interviewed was also coincidentally the best looking: an exotic Eastern European named Milos Sarceev. Milos had a perfectly symmetrical physique and a face like a Slavic angel. Milos said something to me in 1991 that stuck with me to this day. "Marty," he said in his luxurious bohemian accent, "a *real* bodybuilder – you take and lock him in a empty room for twenty minutes – you come back and he has successfully pumped and activated every muscle on his body." Indeed, what could be more *purposefully primitive*, (my code of ethics) than being deprived of all equipment and *still* being able to engage in a productive resistance workout? To Milos, the ability to obtain an effective resistance training workout without equipment was the highest expression of the progressive resistance art.

So when John asked me to review a no-gear dude who had written a book about the whys and wherefores attached to being a personal trainer – my first response was, "Why me?" and without the slightest hesitation Du Cane said, "Because this guy is Gonzo, Marty." Oh, well why didn't you say so earlier? Of course! Being a senior member, a Gonzo OG, requires I extend every courtesy and hospitality to another Gonzo Guild member. And so it came to pass. And, as Du Cane predicted, I loved the book.

Not so much for the content – not that there was anything substandard or insufficient – the essential core of the book is aimed at either being or becoming a better personal trainer. As a fitness cave monk that avoids contact with civilians, that subject matter was of little interest to me – just saying – I do personal training on an extremely limited basis and only with elite athletes. The PT tips, pointers, guidelines, landmines and ways to do better are all in place and discussed with a nice authoritative nonchalance – so that stuff was good – what was better was the vibe, the stance, the tone, the left-field, art school, skateboard, surfer, X-Game Gonzo feel.

Thank f*#king God someone in fitness has a creative streak and is capable of thinking outside the suffocating box of conventional fitness lockstep group thought: guys like the crazed Kavadlo brothers and manic Jim Steel are getting results for clients across the board and all the while maintaining idiosyncratic personalities – they are offbeat dudes using off-beat methods to create renovated humans.

In *The Wild Ones*, 23-year old Marlon Brando is the head of a biker gang razing a town and ravaging the locals. He is asked by a reporter, "What is it, Johnny that you are rebelling against?" Brando says, "What do you got?" Indeed, some of us are born to live a little wild and reckless, past the outer lip of societal norms, ethics and boundaries. The innovators *never* reside inside the box of conventional fitness thinking. Look to the radical thinkers for radical solutions – but caveat emptor! The frauds hide best amongst the freest thinkers.

Danny strikes the right tone: if you are built for it, personal training is one hell-of-a-satisfying career: do it right and you are literally transforming people's bodies and lives. So if you think you're built for it and considering jumping into the shark tank of personal training, I would think this book would be invaluable. And the tattooed Gonzo vibe is priceless.

CHAPTER 1

ONE MAN'S JOURNEY

"WHAT IS THIS THAT
STANDS BEFORE ME?"
-BLACK SABBATH

We are all many things in life. We are different things to different people. To one person, I am a father. To another, a son. We play many roles even within ourselves. We put on different "masks" throughout the days and years of our lives. In fact, if you look at my tattoos (the only thing I get asked about more than my training) you will see that among other themes, masks play a heavy role. Do you wear the same mask around your lover that you do around your boss? Or your mom or best friend for that matter? Who is the Real You, anyway? The same person in the same life can be a student, a friend, a co-worker, a teacher, a neighbor, and yes... a Personal Trainer!

Generations ago, the job you had at age twenty was the job you kept for the rest of your life. You worked into adulthood, doing the same thing again and again and again. Usually the vocation was based either out of necessity or limited choices. If you grew up on a farm and your dad was a farmer, chances are that you would follow in his footsteps. Just one generation ago, if someone was not working at the career of their choice, it was unusual for them to switch jobs past a certain age. People usually stuck with the same occupation day in, day out, again and again, while their body atrophied and their creative juices dried out.   Wake up, work a job you did not choose, sleep because you are dead tired, repeat for the next ten thousand days, retire, and die.

Fortunately, today we have many more career choices available to us.   I oftentimes vent about the crippling effect that technology has on our physical and spiritual health, but I am not unaware of the advantages it plays.   The modern world has made many things more *available* to us. Opportunity is one of those things.

In the grand scheme of things, Personal Trainer is a fairly new profession. It's only in the modern world that one would even need to work out with a fitness professional. Think about it: we were designed to build houses, climb trees, and kill our own beef. These days, however, with most people sitting down fourteen hours a day and believing that cookies made with organic sugar are health food, personal trainers are very much needed.

WE ALL WEAR MANY MASKS

Personal training is one of the most wonderful careers one can get involved in. If you are passionate about fitness and don't wanna sit down for a living, then it's likely you will love being a personal trainer. It does not require much formal education (though street smarts are essential,) you can make a lot of money, and you truly make the world a better place. Some days I cannot believe how lucky I am to be a part of this noble trade. It's a privilege.

PERSONAL TRAINING CLIENTS COME IN ALL SHAPES, SIZES, AND AGES, WITH COMPLETELY VARIED FITNESS LEVELS AND GOALS

Personal training is more than just giving people "lessons" in the gym (or the park, their home, a studio, etc.) Our clients let us into their lives. We see them first thing in the morning. We see them unshowered, unshaven. They let their guard down. Your clients will attempt new things in front of you and only you. Sometimes they succeed; sometimes they fail. You are there for all of it. There is a high level of trust and intimacy.

Personal training clients come in all shapes, sizes, and ages, with completely varied fitness levels and goals, so it is important to note that our job can change week to week, day to day, even hour to hour. We always have to be prepared to go with the flow. At 7 am, you are like a physical therapist, helping an injured victim rehabilitate her knee. At 8:00, you're like a coach preparing an athlete for a match, working on explosive pushups, sprints, and Olympic lifts. At 9:00, you're a therapist listening to your client sort out his family drama, while trying to make sure he manages at least to break a sweat. You get the idea: different things to different people. Just like life. The ability to adapt is necessary.

In The Beginning

When I was a child, I was going to be a rock star. I believed that with more fire and conviction than I have ever believed anything in my life. I had been playing drums since I was eight years old and couldn't imagine doing anything else. In the slight chance that I *wasn't* going to be a rock star, I figured I would at least make a living doing music and nothing else. And believe it or not, I was able to do it for a while. I played in local bands as a kid, went on tour at age 19, and got a record deal at 21. I was living what I thought was the dream. It was great. I was playing 200 shows a year, opening up for my heroes and traveling the world, while making friends and music the whole way through. Until it ended abruptly at the age of 26.

Now what?

WELCOME TO THE 90'S

I had to think fast. I took my experience of being on the road and got hired by an event marketing company to do some grunt-work on one of their traveling productions. Basic stuff like unloading trucks and building stages. I am nothing if not a hard worker. That's part of what has made me a successful trainer.

I worked my ass off and within two years I was in charge of one of the biggest event marketing tours in history, overseeing not only my traveling crew, but over a hundred other employees in various markets across the USA. Here I was, a Brooklyn College dropout, leading a multi-million dollar, nationally-travelling event. One guy who worked for me even had a Masters degree in marketing. This is one of many examples I've come across that highlights how the combination of experience, common sense, and hard work often proves to be a better teacher than any formal "education." The person matters more than the degree.

I was making more money than I ever had before, had the respect of my peers, and I got to travel extensively, but earning a living by selling people on a brand (even a very good brand) left me feeling hollow. Something was missing; it was a sense of purpose, a sense of wanting to make the world a better place. On top of that, my current client was a liquor company hell-bent on advertising to kids (they all do, no matter what they say) and I started to feel like maybe I was making the world even worse. That is when my brother Al suggested to me that I become a Personal Trainer.

Although I had always been seriously into working out, trying every exercise, and reading every workout book I could, a career as a trainer was an option I had never previously entertained. I must say the idea of getting paid to help people get healthy was very appealing to me, especially after making them sick for so long, and the directness and simplicity—just two people in a gym working hard for improvement—was right up my alley. Plus, I wanted to wear sweatpants to work.

It is noteworthy that around this time, I married and impregnated the love of my life, Jennifer. I knew I didn't want to raise my unborn son with the money I earned peddling booze to college kids, but I didn't know what else I could do for us to survive. It was a terrifying conundrum. Do I start over with a new career for the third time, even with a brand new bride and child on the way? Or do I continue to do something I am no longer passionate about? I was starting a family. I needed to be responsible, dammit! I still had twenty-seven years remaining on my mortgage and the economy was about to tank but...

Hey, ya' gotta take a shot!

So at thirty-one years old I made a choice. I was going to be a Personal Trainer.

THE EARLY DAYS OF PERSONAL TRAINING. PICTURED WITH THE TWO PEOPLE WHO MOTIVATE ME MOST.

Enjoy The Ride

I started as an entry-level trainer at a chain health club.   With time, discipline, an open mind, and fierce work ethic, I advanced to Trainer, Master Trainer, and even "Elite Level 5" trainer (more on these terms later.) I worked hard for it. Within two years I was the Personal Training Manager of the gym. It wasn't long before I was promoted to the biggest club in the company. I hired, fired, trained, scheduled, staffed, and managed a team of forty of New York's best personal trainers. I was also accountable for hundreds of clients, most of whom I knew on a first name basis. I always exceeded my annual sales goal of $2.4 million. I set records within that company that remain unbroken and legendary to this day. I won all types of accolades, awards, vacations, and bonuses. I was called upon to mentor other personal trainers, train other managers, recruit for other locations, and lead health fairs for our corporate members. Life was good, but the higher I moved up, the more distance I felt from *actual personal training*!

I had become very far removed from the clients I was trying to help. In the beginning, I set out to be a Trainer not a Manager, and I was once again feeling empty.

So in 2010 I took another chance by leaving one of the most coveted fitness jobs in NYC behind and working independently, or "for self" as we say in Brooklyn.

THE LORD OF
FLATBUSH

In The Present

These days I am fortunate enough to maintain a successful private personal training business and travel yet again, this time leading workshops, certifications, and seminars with my brother Al. It took years of non-stop work and humility to get here. And this is just the beginning.

Prior to becoming a trainer, I had always thought there was some secret, some "trick" too elusive for me to learn. Well, it turns out there are A LOT of secrets. But they're not really tricks; they are time tested methods for which you can manage, grow, and retain your business. What I thought were tricks were actually the collective product of years of practice, education, and lessons shared and learned by those in the personal training community.

Along the way I've been lucky enough to have some of the greatest teachers and mentors in the world. I am happy to pass their wisdom and stories down to you. Use them wisely. This is absolutely not the stuff you learn in personal training school. There will be no anatomy lessons, or sections about stored glycogen. We will not discuss the Karvonan Formula or VO2 Max. Hell, we are not even going to break down specific exercises. There are plenty of books that have that information already. Rather, this is the straight dope on how to start out, how to advance, and how to get paid. So whether you're eighteen years old and this is your first job, or if you've come to it later in life, as so many of us have, I guarantee there will be something here to help you. Even if you've been working as a professional personal trainer for years, there is sure to be wisdom in these pages that will take your career to the next level!

THE GROUND-BREAKING, FIRST EVER PROGRESSIVE CALISTHENICS CERTIFICATION WAS HELD IN JUNE, 2013

I have personally overseen and helped hundreds of trainers in New York City, one of the most competitive markets on the planet, with numerous gyms on every corner and thousands of trainers roaming the streets, thrive by incorporating these methods. I watched their appointment books go from blank to booked in a matter of weeks. I myself have gone from earning $18 paychecks, to being one of America's most in-demand personal trainers simply by doing exactly what this book says.

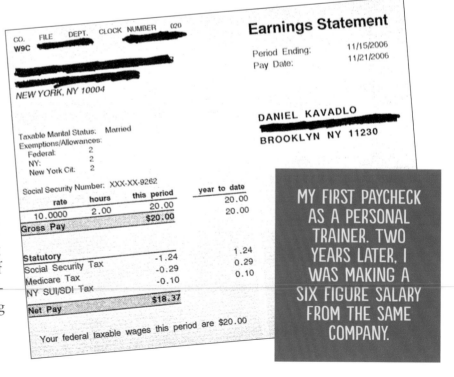

MY FIRST PAYCHECK AS A PERSONAL TRAINER. TWO YEARS LATER, I WAS MAKING A SIX FIGURE SALARY FROM THE SAME COMPANY.

One more thing: Although this book is crammed full of amazing information, it is not a substitute for experience. Nothing is. No book can replace hard work or time. Think of this as a guide containing information that is necessary to advance your career. What you do with it is up to you. The reality of being a personal trainer is nothing like what is promised by fitness schools and institutions. This is the real deal. So if you're willing to swallow a slab of humble pie, strap on your work boots, and *hustle*, then get ready for what can be the most rewarding and thrilling job of your life. Prepare to make a difference, to help people, to change the world!

PREPARE TO MAKE A DIFFERENCE,
TO HELP PEOPLE, TO CHANGE THE WORLD!

That's my experience. I encourage you to have yours.

CHAPTER 2

JOB DESCRIPTION

> "I CAN TURN A JACK AND I CAN LAY A TRACK.
> I CAN PICK AND SHOVEL TOO.
>
> -CAN YOU SWING A HAMMER, BOY?
>
> YES SIR, I'LL DO ANYTHING YOU HIRE ME TO."
> *-JOHNNY CASH,*
> *FROM "THE LEGEND OF JOHN HENRY'S HAMMER"*

I f you're holding this book, chances are you or someone along the way thought you would be great at personal training. They're probably right. That's how it started for me too. It's likely that you already work out and are in better shape than most of your friends, you're good at getting people amped up and have a pleasant demeanor. It wouldn't surprise me if you've already helped one or two of your friends begin a workout program. That is an excellent start. But there is far more to it than that. A personal trainer has many jobs. The following is a general list of some of the most important ones.

MEET THEM, GREET THEM, AND MAKE THE WORKOUT EXPERIENCE LESS FOREIGN TO THEM

Workout Buddy

This is exactly what it sounds like. Before we start out as personal trainers, many of us have it in our minds that we will be working with athletes and fitness enthusiasts. That's what I thought, but it's generally not the case. Although every now and then, a very fit person will hire a trainer, the vast majority of your clientele will be people who never worked out seriously or haven't worked out in twenty years, even if they lead you to believe otherwise. When the prospective client who told you he runs Marathons and usually works out four times a week shows up coughing and can barely walk up a flight of stairs, you will see what I mean.

These people need someone to be there, meet them, greet them, and make the workout experience less foreign to them, almost like a friendly "guide" to working out. That's it. Be their gym buddy. Make it fun. We all perform better with a workout buddy. Think of yourself as a "Stand-In Friend" because none of their real friends will ever join them for a workout. That's why they hired a trainer. Who knows? Maybe you'll even change their lives and give them a love for fitness they never thought was possible. But for now, show up on time, smile, and make sure your client moves. Try your best to help them enjoy the experience. Which leads us to our next role...

IT'S USUALLY HARDER FOR CLIENTS TO DISAPPOINT YOU THAN IT IS TO DISAPPOINT THEMSELVES.

Motivator

The role of Motivator is very near and dear to me. As a matter of fact, I believe it's my biggest strength as a trainer. Being a motivator is a little different than being a workout buddy. Whereas being a workout buddy means that you're providing companionship and guidance, being a motivator requires a little extra proverbial mustard. You need to bring out the best in them. For some of your clients, being a motivator will mean that you (possibly literally) cheer them on as they get their first pull-up. For others it simply means that you provide *accountability,* making sure they show up to train instead of going to the nearest bar or fast food establishment.

To provide the necessary level of motivation for your clients, it is necessary to feel them out. Just as we must step up our motivational game for some, we must recognize the possibility of being too overzealous with others. Read their signals and give them what they need. No matter the type of client, always hold them accountable. You're the trainer. It's usually harder for clients to disappoint you than it is to disappoint themselves.

Psychiatrist

You knew this was coming. In most cases, you will have to, at least occasionally, listen to your clients' problems. You will hear about their jobs, deadlines, relationships, and personal politics. Sometimes, they will even vent about financial concerns. (This is always a tricky situation considering they are paying *YOU*, their trainer, which probably adds to their perceived monetary woes.) I am very much aware that this is not what we had in mind when we signed on for a career in fitness, but I'd like to put a different spin on it: you are here as a health professional. Some say the Body and Mind are connected. I believe that's an understatement; they're actually the *same thing*. Like the ancient proverb says: "Sound body, sound mind." It is likely that when your 6am client vents to you about her asshole boss, she is clearing her mind. Your client is purging her body of anxiety and negativity—essentially *getting healthier*. And you helped them do it! She will probably have that much more energy for the workout now that some stress has been alleviated. The workout will help to expel even more. So be a psychiatrist. Accept it. Your client will still benefit, and ultimately that's your job.

SOME SAY THE MIND AND BODY ARE CONNECTED. I SAY THEY'RE THE SAME THING.

Consultant

Again, it comes back to accountability. But unlike the motivator role we play inside the gym, the consultant helps paying customers stay accountable *outside* of the gym. Let's be honest: it is impossible for a deconditioned individual to get in shape if they train with you for only two hours a week and treat themselves like garbage for the other one hundred and sixty-six. As a trainer, your job can perceivably end when the session is over. But as a consultant, you remind them not to eat those cupcakes at the party. Hell, have them text you from the party to let you know how they did. You want them to think of you when they order a salad instead of fries. Tell your clients to picture you like an angel on their shoulder at the restaurant when they order that salad. This will help them get results, help you retain your client, and therefore make more money. I encourage trainers to make consulting, however formal or informal, a part of every workout.

Sales Person

Let's get this out of the way early on. As professional trainers, we need to get over the notion that charging money for our services diminishes our integrity. Bullshit. If you are not prepared to be a sales person then you are not prepared to be a personal trainer. The sooner you get over this, the better. Doctors charge money. So do plumbers, tattoo artists, hairstylists, and accountants. Even the pope gets paid. This is basic economics. You have to charge money if you need things like food and shoes.

IF YOU ARE NOT PREPARED TO BE A SALES PERSON THEN YOU ARE NOT PREPARED TO BE A PERSONAL TRAINER.

And finally...

Personal Trainer

Your job is to make sure that your clients get a workout that they cannot get without you. Your other job is to build a relationship (more on this in chapter 8.) That's it. Administering a workout that they cannot get without you does not necessarily mean that you provide manual resistance for every single exercise. It doesn't even mean that you spot them on everything. It means that they train harder, *better* when you are there. Maybe it's the truth in your eyes that makes them lock out each of those fifty pushups. Perhaps your words provide the nerve to pull their chin over that sweaty bar. Or maybe it's just the comfort of knowing that you're there for them, which

YOU ARE THERE
FOR YOUR CLIENT.

makes them go that extra inch deeper on every single squat. By contrast, for some folks, simply showing up late, stretching out for twenty minutes, and doing two sets of jumping jacks constitutes a workout that they couldn't do on their own. It is always good to remember that you are there for your client. It's a broad spectrum.

That being said, one person who you are *not* there for is you. If your passion is bodybuilding and a potential client wants to hire a trainer to help him lose his gut or rehab an injury, then do not train him like a bodybuilder. If your possible client wants to lift weights, then your job is to teach him to lift weights with impeccable form, even if you'd rather do MMA-style conditioning drills. Not only is it good customer service to train your client in a way that is appropriate and desirable for them, but you must also accommodate them if you wish to put food on the table. That's right, you gotta eat, and that won't happen if you don't have clients. This is not to say that you can't incorporate exercises that you favor and enjoy. It simply means that you have to put your clients' needs before your own. Trust me, in time, a good trainer finds the balance.

Be Appropriate

Because of my profile in the calisthenics community people are often under the impression that my clients do human flags and muscle-ups all day. That is far from the truth. The overwhelming majority of my business is comprised of working professionals. That's right: store managers, lawyers, teachers, and dentists. Now only after several years, some of my trainees can slay the pull-up bar, but at the beginning, we worked on whatever was appropriate: Proper form, posture, perfect pushups, strengthening the posterior chain, etc. If lunges are more appropriate than pistol squats, then we do lunges. A classic push-up is a better exercise selection for 95% of my clientele than the one-arm variety. Way more people want to train with me because I helped their friend look and feel better, than because they saw my YouTube channel. I am often approached by young trainers who want to know how to get clients. When I ask them how they've gone about achieving this goal so far, they tell me they put a workout video on YouTube. What they should be doing is spending lots of time in the gym talking with potential clients and watching professional trainers make money. They should be working on the most basic of movements, learning to be comfortable on the gym floor, and training with other trainers.

AS MUCH AS I LOVE THE HUMAN FLAG,
IT IS NOT RELEVANT FOR THE VAST MAJORITY
OF PERSONAL TRAINING CLIENTS.

The advice contained in these pages alongside with hard-earned experience will help you start your personal training career better than a thousand YouTube channels or Facebook fan pages. These websites are extraordinary in what they can potentially do, but they are the subject for another book. They will very seldom put you one-on-one in front of potential clients. And they will not make you a good trainer. Be ready to work hard. Consult the equation below:

HOURS + EFFORT = $$$

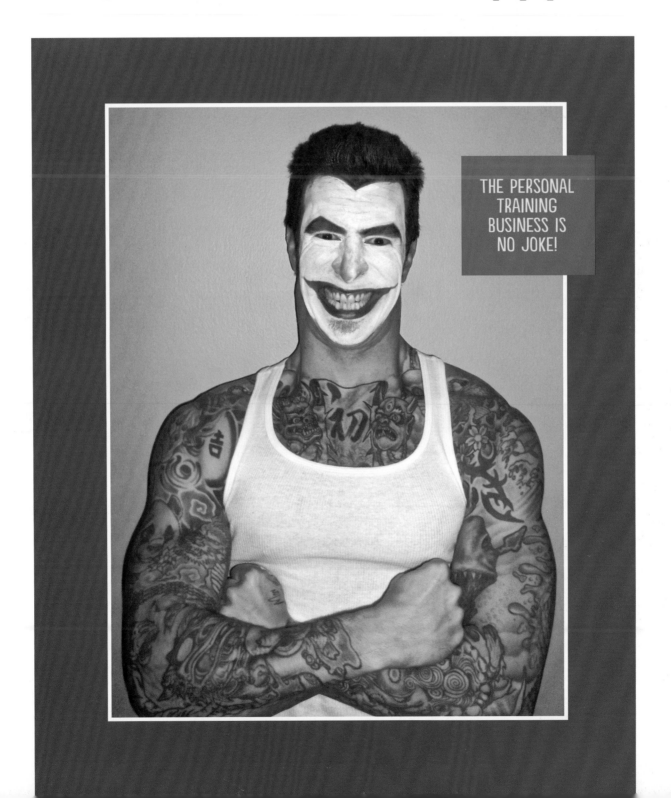

CHAPTER 3

PERSONAL TRAINING
MYTHS EXPOSED

> "BELIEVE NOTHING,
> NO MATTER WHERE YOU READ IT OR WHO
> HAS SAID IT, NOT EVEN IF I HAVE SAID IT,
> UNLESS IT AGREES WITH YOUR OWN REASON
> AND YOUR OWN COMMON SENSE."
> –BUDDHA

Now that we've discussed the truth about being a personal trainer, it is equally important to dispel some of the fiction. The very same people who said you would make a great trainer because of your commitment to fitness and positive attitude probably also told you about some of the perceived advantages. Maybe they have a friend of a friend who supposedly makes a hundred grand a year working part time. Don't believe the hype. There are many myths about being a personal trainer. Here are just a few of the most frequently perpetrated. Let's look at them one at a time:

MYTH #1

"You get to make your own schedule."

As every professional trainer knows, this is complete bullshit. You will have to wake up early. You will sometimes have to wake up in the middle of the night. In fact, in most gyms, 6am-9am is referred to as "peak hours." You will have to work evenings too, as 6pm -9pm is also referred to as "peak hours."

No one gets started as a trainer by picking and choosing their schedule. It is dictated by twenty different people a week: the people you train. Some of them work nights, some work days. Some are parents who wake up at 5am; others are partiers, still boozin' it up at 5am. You have to accommodate all of their schedules, so be prepared to work weekends too. Most personal trainers I know work six or seven days a week.

BE READY
TO RISE
WITH THE
SUN.

MYTH #2

"You can do it on the side."

Just as personal trainers cannot dictate their own schedules, we can't start a career by training "on the side" either. Anyone who has made a long-term career out of personal training will tell you that you can't be picky for years, if ever. Even if your day starts out one way, it can and will morph. A large degree of flexibility and availability is required.

The whole "You are your own boss" mentality needs to be addressed here too. In reality, your client is your boss. They pay your bills. As a PT Manager, I would even tell my staff: "You don't work for me. You don't even work for this gym. You work for your clients." The fact is that if you won't train someone at 5:30am or 10pm, then someone else will. According to the Labor Department, there are over 230,000 personal trainers working in the United States. That number has grown 10% in the last ten years, even as overall employment has declined. Clearly, personal training is one of the country's fastest growing professions; that's probably part of why you're holding this book. It's a competitive market. We trainers do not have the luxury of making all of our decisions.

When I used to interview potential trainers for health clubs, if anyone ever told me that they were interested only in part-time work, I ended the interview. If you're going to do it, commit.

NO! YOU CAN'T DO IT ON THE SIDE.

"Certifications make you a better trainer."

Being a Certified Personal Trainer (CPT) is usually necessary for you to work either directly for, or on the premises of most facilities. So is attending a CPR class. But neither one will make you a better trainer. That's right. Just like getting a learner's permit doesn't mean you suddenly know how to operate a motor vehicle, having a certification doesn't necessarily mean you know how to train. The driver's permit is the paperwork required by the powers that be for you to start learning to drive a car. The CPT is required to start learning to be a trainer, although many have learned to drive or train with neither. It is a mere technicality. Hanging a liquor license on the wall does not mean that the bartender makes a great drink, and taking a "specialty cert" does not always make you a specialist.

There are many certifying bodies. I am certified through the American Council on Exercise (ACE) simply because it is one of the most widely-accepted. ACE, NASM (National Academy of Sports Medicine), NSCA (National Strength & Conditioning Association), and ACSM (American College of Sports Medicine) are a few of the big ones that are accepted just about everywhere. So is a college degree in kinesiology or any type of exercise science.

The fitness industry is rife with excessive caution and esoteric technique. Most certifications have alarmingly few questions about what it's actually like to work as a personal trainer. Generally, there are several questions regarding outdated assessments (Sit and Reach Test, anybody?), gratuitous and rigid pre-workout procedures (way beyond the standard PAR-Q,) and the ever-limited scope of practice (don't suggest any food or supplements, don't try to heal your clients, never give your opinion about anything, etc.) Well I disagree. Common sense is not out of your scope!

Yes, client assessment is a necessary part of being a personal trainer, but the Reagan-era gym class stuff is for the birds. I am of the opinion that you get a better assessment of someone just watching them sit down, stand up, and move. These certifying bodies often require trainers to temporarily memorize complex mathematical formulas and fake ethical scenarios, both of which are irrelevant in the real world. There's no way to decisively prove if any of these formulas have any weight (who says a fifty-year-old's heart rate should not surpass 170 bpm?) Often the situations presented on these exams are more about semantics and HR code than integrity.

PAR-Q

Par-Q stands for Physical Activity Readiness Questionnaire and is designed to help you help yourself. There are tremendous benefits associated with staying involved in a regular exercise program. Completing the PAR-Q is a sensitive step to take prior to increasing the amount or intensity of physical activity in your life.

For most people physical activity should pose no hazard. Par-Q will help identify the small number of individuals who should receive medical advice concerning the type and intensity of exercise suitable for them.

Simply use your common sense and circle "Y" or "N" for each of the following questions:

Has a doctor ever told you that you have heart trouble?   Y   N

Do you frequently have pains in your heart or chest?   Y   N

Do you feel faint or have spells of severe dizziness?   Y   N

Has a doctor ever told you that you blood pressure is unsafely high?   Y   N

Has a doctor ever told you that you have a bone or joint problem that has been aggravated by exercise?   Y   N

Is there a good physical reason not mentioned here why you should not follow an activity program?   Y   N

Are you over the age of 65 and not accustomed to physical movement?   Y   N

It is recommended that you consult with a physician before embarking on an exercise program if you've answer Yes to one or more of the above questions.

Print Name_____   Date_____

Signature_____

PAR-Q STANDS FOR PHYSICAL ASSESSMENT READINESS QUESTIONNAIRE. I DON'T ADVISE ASKING ANY MORE THAN THIS WITHOUT BEING GIVEN A REASON.

To maintain your CPT cert, you will take continuing education credits. This can be done online or in person. I strongly encourage you to take an in-person workshop or seminar on material that interests you. If a fitness pro you admire is instructing in your area, then by all means attend. Not only will it be fun and exciting, you will probably gain more from it because of the very fact that it is of interest to you. (The alternative to attending a workshop is usually spending twenty hours studying theoretical information on a screen.)

Of course, workshops can potentially be disappointing too. I took a low-budget kettlebell "certification" several years ago which not only failed to teach proper technique, but taught explicitly *wrong* technique. Today I would be embarrassed by simply watching a trainer use the form I learned in that class. Like everything, some seminars are excellent; others are complete crap. Make sure you go with someone you trust. But no course of any kind is a substitute for putting in the time on the training floor if you want to be a career trainer.

Some of the greatest and most established trainers I know have never been certified.

MYTH #4

"You will be promoted based on your education."

That's right; this is a myth too. Not only do most commercial continuing education programs do nothing to make you a better trainer, they do not make you command a higher rate either. No matter what the gym literature says, trainers are promoted by their ability to make money. "Junior," "Entry-Level," and "Level 1" trainers are all the same thing: trainers who have few or zero clients. A level 1 trainer could have numerous credentials or could have dropped out of third grade. He is Level 1 because he is willing to work for less than the in-demand trainers.

Saying that trainers are promoted based on their education is a great selling tool for the gym. It helps to sell members on personal training ("Ohhh," you can imagine them saying, "My trainer is Power-Plate certified. He's so educated.") But it also sells you, the trainer, on continuing certifications ("If I spend more money on certifications, I will make more money.") FALSE!

Supply and demand really dictate levels. Your boss will promote you when he or she sees that clients are willing to pay more for you. Trainers are promoted to "Master," "Elite-Level" or "Level 5" trainers only when they sell lots of sessions and are booked extensively. If you want a higher rate, then be available, work hard, and acquire clients. Make your time valuable.

"You will pick up clients quickly."

This is one of the biggest whoppers of them all. At first, almost no one will want to train with you, even if they say otherwise. I will never forget my first interview for a personal training job. It was a Monday. I had just left an upper-level management position in event marketing on Friday. I wasn't completely surprised that the gentleman interviewing me only had one question. After all, I came highly recommended and I showed up on time. It's what he asked me that shocked me.

"Why on earth would you want to be a trainer?"

It was one of the few times in my life I was ever caught off guard. "Why would he ask me that?" I said to myself. Without giving much thought, I answered something like "To get people in great shape and make the world a better place!" While my reply was 100% true, it was very idealistic. Like many, I assumed that if I worked at a gym, there would automatically be people there for me to train. I didn't think about the process. I needed to supplement my idealism with realism.

It's not as easy as many people think it is to get hard-working folks to spend their cash on you. Be prepared to be broke for a few months. It's called paying your dues. If you are diligent, professional, and bust your ass, this phase will pass. It is extraordinarily rare that someone says "Gee, I feel like hiring a trainer today." It almost never happens, so don't count on it ever happening. No one will walk up to you and say "Hey, I want to train with you." However, just about *everyone* who walks up to you will *potentially* train with you. It is on you to establish the need. Show them how personal training can help them reach their goals. Prove that working out can be fun, not intimidating. Help them see how much better they will feel all the time if they start a program with you now. They don't know this. You have to show them.

I have been thanked by dozens of people for "talking them into personal training." They were in the best shape of their lives, and grateful to me for it. In reality however, all I did was help them tap into something that was already there. You have to make them "decide" to do it. Everybody needs training. Part of your job is to help these good people see that.

YOU HAVE TO ESTABLISH THE NEED.

MYTH #6

"Being a good athlete means you'll be a good trainer."

Something that put me on the fence about starting a career in personal training was that I did not have what on paper would be called an "athletic background." Yes, I had been committed to fitness and health for decades: I worked out effectively and consistently, cooked my own clean food, and tried to do good things for the people around me. But in my first training job, I worked alongside Marathon runners, MMA fighters, and a professional rugby player. These cats were actual athletes!

The funny thing is, in many ways I was more qualified to train a normal person than any of these guys were. I could relate better. Like the gym patrons, I was doing other things with my teens and twenties than competing athletically. And now, here I was, a man in my thirties (another entry-level trainer hired at the same time was nineteen) who had a job and a kid, yet was still in fantastic shape! I was a better fit for the prospective clients. They didn't want to fight in a steel cage; they just want to look better with their shirts off. Besides, real fighters don't hire personal trainers at trendy East Village spas. They can't afford it.

MANY SUCCESSFUL TRAINERS HAVE A BACKGROUND IN THE ARTS.

Many successful trainers I've known have had backgrounds in the arts. I've seen former actors, dancers, and musicians *kill it* in the training universe. Perhaps after working hard for so long and being exploited as an artist, being exploited as a trainer doesn't seem so bad. (That was a joke, sort of.)

I have also noticed that both former military and former inmates can transition into being successful trainers. Perhaps it's because both groups are conditioned to waking up early and respecting a chain of command. As a fitness manager, some of the best hires I ever made have had a past.

Just to be clear about something, I am not saying that athletes don't make phenomenal personal trainers. A lot of the time, they do. What I am saying is that being a successful trainer is a different skill than being an athlete and there is not always an overlap.

MYTH #7

"You have to look like a body builder to be a successful trainer."

I must confess that even I bought into this one at first. When we start out a new career as a trainer (or anything else) we are often insecure.   Am I good enough? Strong enough? Fit enough?

Well, probably... Yes. Maybe I don't look like a body builder, but it turns out that most of my clients and prospective clients do not want me to. They don't want themselves to either. There are many physiques of trainers, from lean and sinewy, to short and squat, and everything else in between. I have even seen heavyset trainers succeed. Although I would never personally hire one (you gotta practice what you preach!) I have known several ample-bodied individuals who have dominated the personal training world. There is no archetype of what a personal trainer's body should be.

THERE IS NO ARCHETYPE OF WHAT A PERSONAL TRAINER'S BODY SHOULD BE.

MYTH #8

"It's smooth sailing once you build a client base."

Make no mistake. No matter how good of a trainer you are, your best client will leave you in time. Eventually, they will move, start a family, stop giving a shit, or lose their job. Like Edward Norton says in the motion picture *Fight Club*, "On a long enough timeline, the survival rate for everyone drops to zero." This is especially true for your clients. The personal training industry therefore is driven by new business. Whether you work for a chain gym or for yourself, you must put time into getting new clients. Hand out cards or fliers, talk to the gym members, hype your services, and ask for referrals. Don't rest on your laurels. Hustle.

MYTH #9

"Personal trainers are interchangeable."

This myth is often perpetrated by the fitness industry itself. The big chain gyms want the clients to think that one trainer can be easily swapped for another. As long as they're wearing a trainer shirt, then they're all the same, like a worker at McDonald's. But this is not true. Remember to always sell the client on *you*.

Generally, the industry wants us (the trainers) to believe this myth too. But there are many types of trainers and many types of training. Although we want to be as diverse and qualified as possible, no one can be everything to everybody. We are all different; that's what makes life beautiful. Never forget that it's called *personal* training not *robot* training.

THERE ARE MANY TYPES OF PERSONAL TRAINING.

"You will get laid all the time."

I really contemplated omitting this one entirely, but my job in writing this book is to help with being a professional personal trainer in the real world, so I must address it. Maybe some of you have heard the expression "Don't shit where you eat." Or at least "Do not mix business with pleasure." Well, that is absolutely the case here.

I understand that the fitness industry is an extremely sexually-charged business. I won't deny it. One need look no further than contemporary marketing for evidence ("Look better naked" from David Barton Gym is one of the best examples.) And yes, if you are working as a personal trainer, you probably work out and care about your appearance. It is likely that your personal training peers do too. We don't need to be scientists to know what happens when you put like-minded, attractive people in a situation where they're exhibiting their bodies in an intimate and physical environment. All I can say is don't take the bait. I have seen fitness professionals "resign" from top-level positions because they made foolish choices at work.

Don't fuck your clients either. The gym may get sued. You may get sued. You will almost certainly lose your job. But aside from that, you will definitely lose the client. The relationship will change. So ask yourself why you're in the gym. Is it to meet people or is it to have a successful, lucrative, long-term career? There are enough men and women in the world that we don't need to shit where we eat. Make love somewhere else. Make money in the gym.

CHAPTER 4

THE HEALTH CLUB

> "YOU CAN FIND ME IN THE CLUB,
> BOTTLE FULL OF BUB."
> -CURTIS "50 CENT" JACKSON, FROM "IN DA CLUB"

hen talking about health clubs, I am referring to large gyms with many members and employees. They are often, but not always chains. You may hear them referred to as "big box gyms." We are all familiar with this type of facility. It's the kind of place you probably picture when someone says "I'm gonna join the gym."

In my opinion the health club is the best place for a new trainer to get started. Some trainers continue to thrive and prosper in the same club for years, even decades. There is nowhere that you will learn the law of the jungle like you will in a big box gym. Some of these places are teeming with industry veterans, all types of trainers, and some of the world's best sales people. Of course, there are also scam artists, horrible sales people, and incompetent trainers, but like in most industries, the cream of the crop will rise to the top. With so many characters, you will see an unbelievable turnover of gym employees. Often, the busier the gym, the faster the turnover. Eventually you will see who the big players are: the membership reps who sell everybody a two-year paid-in-full with personal training, the trainers who are booked all day long with new and returning business, and the managers that last more than three months. If you are new, then watch and learn. The right health club can be an amazing opportunity for you.

Introduce Yourself

Simply being in the presence of more experienced trainers and absorbing their vibe will make you a better trainer through osmosis alone. Spend time in the gym. Learn the craft like an old school apprentice. Showing respect and a sound work ethic will make others more receptive to you, but there is no substitute for time. It's like they say, "You wanna be a monk, you gotta make a lot of rice." Being a trainer means making a lot of rice.

Walk around, introduce yourself and shake every single trainer's hand on your first day. Be sure to greet the non-personal training staff too. Put out the right energy, be professional, yet humble, and many of the big dogs will be happy to help you if you have questions. The wisest trainers will want to see you improve. They know that anything that promotes and sells personal training is good. For example, if I sign up a client right now, then every other trainer in the gym looks good to every single member. Why? Because it shows that personal training is a valuable commodity. The more people buy it, the more others want it. Nothing attracts a crowd like a crowd.

When I started out and introduced myself to everybody, I was greeted with a warm reception overall. However, two of the veteran trainers did not like a rookie who could train his ass off, pick up clients off the floor, and work all hours with boundless energy and vitality. These two let their grievances be known. Mouthing off to their own clients (some of whom were paying over $100 per hour, mind you) about how I sucked, or throwing baby tantrums at meetings about how things are unfair, were business as usual for these elite fitness professionals. To be honest, I really did not care what they thought of me; my work spoke for itself. I wasn't there to make friends.

I was there to, as my son says, "make money and muscles!" The truth is that having me on their team actually made these chumps look good; they just couldn't see it. The only ones responsible for making them look bad were themselves. It is an interesting footnote that years later, one of these goofballs finally admitted to me that I knew "how to sell." A small victory… I'll take it! He subsequently wound up getting fired for allegedly selling illegal substances out of his locker. These days, we're cool with each other. It wasn't until I became the other one's boss that he meekly extended his hand toward mine and suggested we bury the hatchet. I gladly obliged and went on to help him make a lot more money. No hard feelings!

I did not focus on the negative, only on the task at hand. I put in the time and focused my energy toward becoming a better trainer and improving my income. Like an old school apprenticeship, getting started at a gym requires you to put in time. It takes hours and years to pick up the subtleties of the craft. A quality gym can be a cornerstone in building a spectacular career if you are prepared to learn, work hard, and check your ego from time to time.

Of course there is a downside…

The "Pimp/Ho" Relationship

Being employed as a personal trainer at a health club puts you in front of more prospective clients than working just about anywhere else. In a city like New York, it is not unusual for a trainer at such an establishment to be exposed to hundreds of paying members within a single 3-hour primetime shift. Although these gyms usually charge fair rates for personal training, they take a huge cut. Who said pimpin' ain't easy?

The numbers vary, but most trainers make far less than half of what the gym charges. Also, in most cases, trainers don't get paid at all unless they are in a paid session. In other words, with most gyms, when no one is paying to train with you, you are not getting paid. That means all that time on the floor learning the ropes, picking up weights, and soliciting potential clients is free. That's fine. If you put in your time and employ the teachings of this book and of fellow trainers, you will turn that effort into paid production hours.

On the flip side, some gyms do offer compensation (usually around minimum wage) for "floor shifts." Floor shifts require, rather than encourage, you to be present in the gym without clients. Although this sounds better than the alternative above, be cautious of this situation. Make sure the gym allows you to pick up new clients during your shift. If they do not, then it's not worth it. That's the main reason to be there. If your floor shift is 6pm-9pm, then you will make a lot less in three hours than you would in one paid production hour. Also, take into consideration that the gyms that pay out for floor shifts usually pay out less than the others do for production hours (actual paid personal training.)

The essence of the Pimp/Ho relationship is that in exchange for permission to let you work their territory, the pimp takes most of your money. It still makes sense to start at a club. It's much harder to get new clients and learn the business anywhere else.

Get That Money

Training in a big gym means no travel time between appointments and an opportunity for new business every single day. It also means meeting new members who, on some level, just now decided to change their life. Most gyms offer new or renewing members some sort of "trial workout" or "fitness evaluation." These are excellent opportunities to get new business. The trial sessions are called "assessments" because no one would come to them if we called them "sales pitches."

I call them "First Workouts." It's appropriate and has a nice ring to it. It implies that there will be more workouts to come. I never call it "free." I don't recommend using the word "free" in association with your personal training ever. The word "free" communicates to your prospective clients (PC's) that your services have no value. That is the opposite of what you want to show them. In fact, you want them to pay for more sessions after this initial one. Say it's included with the member ship; say it's on you; say it's a valuable service provided to new members; say they won a damn contest; say anything! Just not "free." I don't even like "complimentary." Your time is valuable. Don't let your pimp tell you otherwise.

1. Make The Phone Call

It is tempting to reach out via text message or email, but I strongly encourage you to call. It builds familiarity right off the get-go. Remember, personal training is all about relationships. A human voice is more intimate than a text from a stranger. The call is often a lot more efficient than texting as well. What can take a series of multiple texts to communicate can often be said in a one-minute conversation. While it's true that much of the time the PC won't pick up the phone, it's still good to call anyway. If they do pick up, it is a golden opportunity. With a live voice on the phone, the two of you can begin building a relationship immediately. If they do not pick up, then leave a message. Keep it friendly, terse, and concise. Feel free to text or email in addition to, but not instead of leaving a voicemail. My standard message was something like this:

> *"Hi Joe. This is Danny your personal trainer calling from Big Box Gym. I'm calling to welcome you on board and confirm our first session together tomorrow at 12. I'll meet you by the front desk. I'm really looking forward to meeting you! I can be reached at ------- if you need to get a hold of me. See you tomorrow at noon."*

Have a friendly tone, use the client's first name, and ask the right (open-ended) questions. The purpose of the phone call is not just to confirm the appointment. It is to establish yourself as someone the PC wants to be around. It is often your first chance to make an impression.

Be articulate. Practice speaking the words before you call. I have witnessed phone calls handled both brilliantly and abominably.

BE ARTICULATE. PRACTICE SPEAKING THE WORDS BEFORE YOU CALL.

2. Be At Least 5 Minutes Early

Sadly, punctuality is a skill lacking in many professional personal trainers. It is impossible for me to overstate the incredible importance of being a little early and not having to rush. If it takes you forty-five minutes to commute to the gym, then allow an hour. Why leave things to chance? You will be less stressed, conduct higher quality sessions, and have a better relationship with your clients.

In addition to being five minutes early, be exactly where you said. It's not enough to simply be in the building. Your client may not know what you look like or feel comfortable enough to ask. If you said you'll be by the front desk, then be by the front desk. Have your jacket off and be ready for the session. It would be nice if you had a towel for them too. Maybe even a bottle of water. You're here for them; show it! The "Be At Least 5 Minutes Early" rule is not limited to first workouts. It applies to all PT sessions and everything else in life. It's part of the formula for success.

BEING EARLY FOR EVERYTHING IS PART OF THE FORMULA FOR SUCCESS.

3. Ask The Right Questions

The workout is all about the person you are training. You need to find out what he or she is looking for. You also want them to feel comfortable with you. One of the best ways is to ask a lot of questions. The term "open-ended" is used in sales quite frequently. It refers to questions that don't have a "yes" or "no" answer. These questions get the prospect talking. Find out about them. Who are they? Why are they here? I used to start out my first workouts by asking "Why did you join the gym?" The PC would usually say something about wanting to get in better shape, to which I would simply reply "What does that mean... to you?" I asked open-ended questions because I wanted to start building a bond with them right there. I wanted them to keep talking.

We in the industry can take it for granted that we talk about fitness all day. Many of your PCs are not comfortable telling someone they just met that they need to lose forty pounds, or that they get out of breath when walking to the subway (or the nearest Subway restaurant.) It's hard stuff for most people to share so it takes a fair amount of trust for them to open up to you; this can be prompted by the right questions. The more they tell you, the better. The relationship starts.

4. Make Bold Statements

At one or more points in the workout, you are going to make a bold statement. There are many kinds of bold statements.

Sometimes a bold statement is simple: "You're gonna feel great after we lose this baby-weight." ("We," never "you.")

Bold statements can be silly, even audacious: "Picture it... the crystal clear waves crashing across your chiseled, sculpted calves as the Pacific sun beats down on the ripped abs we've created!"

They can be direct: "Dude, you're looking much better. I'm sure the women are noticing. This summer's gonna be awesome!"

And yes, sometimes they are serious: "You gotta change your life or you're gonna have a heart attack."

Oftentimes, health clubs like your bold statements to be completely over-the-top. I once had a PT Manager who had a contest among new trainers: The trainer who made the most absurd bold statement was declared the winner. Of course, the gym was the real winner as revenue spiked from a direct result of all the bold statements!

But sales aside, making a bold statement actually helps your client. It is possible that he or she never thought about the outcome of training in these terms. It's good for your clients to visualize goals. You are their guide to fitness. Let them know you are there to help them see it through.

I still make bold statements all the time. But instead of telling the PC how beautiful she's gonna look in her wedding dress (the go-to example for selling PT in many corporate sales manuals,) I explain that it's a long road that I'm prepared to walk with her. We can achieve anything together but it will take hard work and discipline. We'll have to earn it.   I tell the PC "You will have to do your part both with me and on your own. It won't be easy but it will be worth it, and if we make the right effort, we cannot fail!" It's okay to be over the top but it's still important to tell the truth.

5. Do The Right Thing

If you do not know for sure that the workout is going great, then ask. Oftentimes trainers are so concerned with coming off like an expert that they lose sight of why they're here. (Hint: we're here for the client.) I have seen some trainers try so hard to have an answer for every question and a go-to program for every person. The truth is that it's impossible to know the perfect program (is there such a thing anyway?) for everybody, especially after just meeting them. You will always have to improvise. On a first workout, halfway through, simply ask some version of "Is this what you were looking for?" Or "Is there anything you wanted to work on that we haven't checked out yet?" The late, great Ed Koch, New York City's quintessential mayor, was famous for asking "How'm I doin'?" I encourage you to do the same during a first workout. In sales, this is called a "Trial Close."

"HOW'M I DOIN?"

6. Sell It

Don't expect the client to say YES to training unless you explicitly ask for the sale. Seriously, the number one reason that trainers miss out on sales is because they do not ask for them. You have to let them know that this is a service that you charge for and that it is in their best interest to continue. Never lie, mislead, or make false promises, but do be confident. (See Chapter 12 for more on sales.)

Live Long And Prospect

The term "prospecting" refers to walking the training floor, and interacting with members, the goal being client acquisition. No place literally puts you in front of more potential clients than a busy gym. The people there spend money on fitness. They paid for gym memberships. They paid for exercise clothes, a locker, and a smoothie. Maybe they will pay for a trainer too. That's up to you.

Sometimes trainers think that prospecting simply means correcting someone's form on a particular exercise. That's hard to do without coming across like a know-it-all. Like a first workout, open ended questions are good for prospecting. Maybe ask them why they're doing a particular exercise in the first place. Offer them an alternative. Ask them about their sneakers or the song on the radio. Smile. Make eye contact. Be pleasant. Let them know you are there for them.

Ask if they've ever worked with a trainer. If they are currently with a trainer at your gym, then tell them what a great choice they made and walk away. It's never okay to prospect another trainer's client, but being friendly is always good. The more communication and comfort there is between all trainers and trainees, the more personal training is promoted throughout the club. The clients will feel like they're part of the scene. Be cool to all of them. In all honesty, with the staff turnover rate so high at the clubs, they may become your client anyway if their trainer leaves or gets fired.

If the prospect is not working with a member of your team, then schedule an appointment. Remember, the workout you offer them is never "free." It's included in their membership or it's your treat. People don't want to pay for something that they were told costs nothing. We've all heard the phrase "Why buy the cow when you get the milk for free?"

Book it, get the PC's info, write the appointment down for them, and follow standard first workout protocol. (See Appendix A.) If they say no to a workout, then book a "tentative" one. Get the info, write it down, and make the phone call.

A trainer I know named Tony (who inspired the title of this book) picked up one client a day for twenty days in a row by prospecting in this method. He became a top trainer in record time. He'd prospect at the front desk, the gym floor, fitness classes, and the juice bar. He never made excuses and took advantage of the fact that big box gyms are teaming with possible clients. Do not expect anyone to get clients for you. Like in life, you are accountable for your own fate. The opportunity is there for the taking. Get it.

Out Of The Box Prospecting

Setting up a Body Fat analysis station is a great way to meet prospective clients. Even though those body fat readers are not accurate, they do provide an ice-breaker when

approaching new people. When I used this method in the early days, I would strike up a conversation about anything from sports to food to music, even about the fact that body fat readers don't work! From there, we would move the conversation to things that do work, like personal training, and schedule a first workout. Everybody needs training... bad!

Do Your Job

Despite some of the negatives of working at a big box gym (the pimp/ho relationship instantly comes to mind), I stand firmly with the clubs on one thing: If you work at a gym, then do your job. If it requires you to fill out a daily client log, then do it. If you must wear a uniform, then wear it. If meetings are mandatory, then attend them. If you don't want to do something that is part of your job description, then seek employment elsewhere. I'm all about sticking it to the man, but I did every job I was ever hired to do to the best of my ability. Don't sign on unless you are prepared to do what is required of you.

IF WEARING A UNIFORM IS PART OF YOUR JOB THEN DO IT.

Let's Get Hired

Start off by getting certified through an organization like ACE, NASM, or ACSM. Get CPR certified through the American Red Cross. I advise taking care of these tasks before seeking a job, as they can be more time consuming than many people think. Although there is no correlation between getting certified and being a good trainer, certification will help you land a job more quickly.

Make a resume. Include your name, phone number, and email. Resume writing, like personal training, is a skill unto itself, but there are some guidelines with which you just can't go wrong. Keep the font clear, clean, and easy to read. Bold holds. Include relevant work experience only. In the days when I hired trainers constantly, it was a big turn-off to look at someone's acting resume when I wanted a trainer. Still, keep in mind that relevant experience is not limited to the fitness industry, and is inclusive of sales jobs, teaching positions, physical labor, military experience, and more. My marketing background actually helped me get hired. It was relevant. The interviewer said "Wow, you probably shook more hands than anyone I've ever interviewed." He was thrilled to give me a shot in spite of the fact that I had no personal training experience. Remember that the only point of the resume is to help facilitate you getting the job. Only include information that will help with that goal and don't let the resume exceed one page. Now print out a few copies on good old-fashioned paper.

I do not recommend seeking a personal training position via the internet. It is impossible to make the same impression as you would in person. Besides, managers want to see that you can hustle. No matter what anybody says, sitting at home by a computer emailing Craig's List postings is not hustling. If you want a job, get up, leave the house, and shake some hands. I discarded 100% of the resumes I received via email, but I looked at every single one that was hand delivered. I was only interested in trainers with the confidence for an in-person experience.

When you seek a job, it's important to look sharp. Although there is no reason to wear a suit to the gym, I encourage you to wear clean, flattering clothes. Workout gear is great; just make sure you look good. Try to imagine the way Hugh Jackman or Michelle Obama's trainer would dress. Walk into the gym clean-smelling, with teeth freshly brushed. Introduce yourself with a big smile and a handshake. Look people in the eye and be articulate. Ask who to speak to about a personal training job. Don't be in a rush; you may have to wait. If you're lucky enough to meet the person who does the hiring, introduce yourself and shake their hand. Show energy, professionalism, and positivity. Anyone who hires you will want to see that you are comfortable with people and not unpleasant to be around. Here's your chance. If they can't meet you on the spot, then schedule an interview, to which you will show up a minimum of five minutes early.

The main point of the interview will be to see that you can be on time and professional. It is important to remember that you are not interviewing the gym; they are interviewing you. Sometimes trainers fresh out of fitness school think that because they just spent a lot of money on a certification, that any gym would be lucky to hire them. (Fitness schools encourage this fiction to justify their rates, but it's not so.) Show how it would help them to hire you. If you made money for past employers, then say so. If you've never been late in your life, say that too. Let them know about how you helped a friend lose weight. Be respectful and considerate, but sell yourself. The ability to sell oneself is a trait all personal trainers need.

If you are unable to schedule an interview or a time to return, then ask with whom you can leave a resume. Get the name of the person and thank them, using their name. Get the business card or direct extension of the PT Manager. Call the next day to make sure they got your resume. Or better yet, stop in and introduce yourself again.

Being a good trainer means following up and following through. Most PT Managers will appreciate someone who is forthcoming and consistent when seeking a job. Those are some of the characteristics they want in their trainers. I once hired an inexperienced trainer (who I had serious second thoughts about) solely because she kept coming back again and again. That's the only reason. Eventually I interviewed her, figuring that almost anyone can learn the science of being a trainer, but you can't buy that type of determination. She is still one of the top trainers at that gym.

Follow up all interviews and conversations with a phone call or visit. Always keep things on positive terms whether you get the job or not. Good luck!

CHAPTER 5

THE BOUTIQUE GYM

"LUXURY MUST BE COMFORTABLE,
OTHERWISE IT IS NOT LUXURY."
-COCO CHANEL

The boutique gym is an attractive, high-end alternative to the big box. Boutiques (or personal training studios) tend to offer the best in amenities (towel service, luxury shower heads, quality toiletries) and are usually much cleaner and better maintained than their larger, more commercial counterparts. They tend to offer greater privacy and better customer service as well. Affluent, affable people go to these studios to avoid the crowds and work one-on-one with their personal trainers. Much of the time, these facilities do not even offer memberships without personal training. If they do, it is usually in a limited capacity. These gyms don't get packed during peak hours and have a very different feel from the big clubs, usually calmer and less chaotic.

Many trainers seek employment at these studios under the assumption that they will earn more than they can at a health club. They think that because they perceive the members of this posh, eucalyptus-scented environment to be rich, that it will automatically transfer over to them. Well, as we have already discussed, you can't count on anyone but yourself for business (or anything else,) not even the high-end studio. You may think the members are rich, but I'll bet most of them would not describe themselves as such. Like at the big health club, your success will always come down to you and only you.

For Better Or For Worse

The relationship between the trainers, members, and staff at the boutique studio is not the same as it is at the big club. The high-end studio is more intimate. Unlike the big box gyms which are rife with politics, cliques, and tension, the trainers at the boutiques make up a smaller group. They're generally there to make their money, take a workshop, or work out. Also, there tends to be fewer trainers who get easily threatened by any perceived disturbance to their territory (other trainers.) The clients are often more respectful too.

As an employee, you are treated slightly better than at the big club. Fewer co-workers and members usually equate to better service and a happier staff. Unfortunately, it also means a lot fewer prospective clients. You have to take the good with the bad.

The relationship between employer and trainer in this situation is less "Pimp/Ho" than at the health clubs. This time, it's more of a "Madame/High-Priced Call Girl" relationship. At the boutique, your boss is often the actual owner of the studio, not a manager appointed by a CEO you never see. Again, like the extra intimacy provided by a smaller studio environment, this is mostly a good thing, but not without a few negatives. On one hand, he or she is probably a fitness professional who decided not to work for someone else. That's pretty cool in itself. As independent businesses owners tend to treat their employees more humanely than the larger corporations do, you will probably notice a less rapid turnover of staff than at the big clubs. On the other hand, it's harder to qualify for things like bonuses and health care in a small, independent place.

The owners of the high-end studios are often trainers too. That is excellent for many reasons. You will indubitably have more in common with a boss who is a fellow trainer than one who is a corporate stooge. The trickle-down effect comes straight from the top, so there will probably be greater concern for individual clients and better workouts than you would experience with the "churn 'n burn" ideology of the big chains. It's good when your boss is a trainer. There is solidarity among trainers. Brotherhood. Empathy. Compassion.

The bad part is that your boss will probably keep all the best clients for him- or herself.

The reason they do this is because they meet all the members first. Studio owners are experienced trainers who know who the big spenders are, and most of the time, they assess and sell everybody themselves. They handle all first workouts. Why wouldn't they? It is the studio owner's personal business and he doesn't want to leave the crucial sales process in the hands of anyone else. I'd do the same.

A Different Kind Of First Workout

Most of the first workouts that you will perform in this type of gym have already been sold training. That's right; it's usually a paid session. Members who sign up for personal training at the same time that they purchase their membership are called "point-of-sale" clients. Although this does happen at big clubs (especially with a competent PT Manager,) it is much more likely in a boutique. The client comes to you having already bought sessions. Sounds great, doesn't it?

But the frequency is low and it can take a long time to build a client base through point-of-sale alone. Chances are that most of the new clients you get were passed down to you simply because the owner or manager couldn't fit the appointments into his or her own schedule. That is how you get most of your clients in the boutique studio.

On the flipside, sometimes boutiques really appreciate a qualified trainer joining the team. A well-established trainer might be able to walk in and get handed a full book of clients if the owner is confident in the trainer's ability to retain them. Remember, just because the owner cannot train every member of the gym personally, they still want to keep the business. Show them you can do it for them. Give solid, confident work-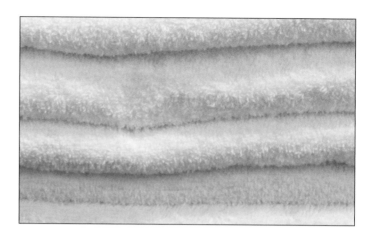
outs, and build relationships. Practice the teachings in this book.

Referrals are seldom in the studio and prospecting is a whole other story...

Slim Pickins

The chances of picking up new clients from prospecting in a personal training studio rest somewhere between slim and none. In fact, most of these facilities would prefer that you do not prospect their members. These members paid for top level service and probably don't want to be harassed by a new trainer in search of business, whereas members of the big chains half-expect it.

The other reason that it's next to impossible to prospect in the boutique is that everyone is already with a trainer! It would be inappropriate to prospect there. However, still be friendly and helpful to all. Although the trainer turnover rate is not as quick as at the big clubs, it's still faster than in most other industries. Any client can potentially become yours should their current trainer leave.

The Low End Theory

A phenomenon that's been surfacing with increased frequency is something that can only be described as a "low budget boutique." They are just like the others, but they cost less. As you may imagine, they are generally not as clean or hospitable. Often, the staff cares less and works less hard than at the nicer places.

People go to low budget boutiques because they know the importance of working with a personal trainer and they want a bargain.

Naturally, these low budget personal training studios pay their trainers much less than the high-end places do. They sometimes pay less than the big box chains as well. The best trainers do not work cheap for very long, so the members who signed up just to save money often wind up selling themselves short.

Size Matters

Any way you slice it, there is a much smaller pool to sell to. But although there are less business opportunities, you can still make a very good living in this environment. In fact, it is arguable that the higher quality of the potential clients more than makes up for the lower quantity. Half the members of big box gyms stop coming after a week. The retention at the studio tends to be much higher.

If you know how to give a great workout and are prepared to put in the time, you can be wildly successful and dominate the studio. You won't be able to get business nearly as fast as my man Tony can by offering training sessions to everyone in a busy club, but you *can* get the business. It will just take longer. Work hard and do the best with what you got. I have some very close friends that have long-standing positions as top level trainers at some of New York City's most elite, high-end gyms. They are the first to admit that it usually takes a lot longer to establish a full appointment book, but they also believe that due to the positive environment, the focus on personal training, and the caliber of the clients, it is 100% worth any sacrifice.

> IF YOU KNOW HOW TO GIVE A GREAT WORKOUT AND ARE PREPARED TO PUT IN THE TIME, YOU CAN BE WILDLY SUCCESSFUL AND DOMINATE THE STUDIO.

CHAPTER 6

YOUR PT MANAGER

"TO PUNISH ME FOR MY CONTEMPT FOR AUTHORITY,
FATE MADE ME AN AUTHORITY MYSELF."
-ALBERT EINSTEIN

The person who hires you in the club is the Personal Training Manager. Sometimes this person is also a trainer, a membership consultant, or even the General Manager, but in the larger clubs, PT Manager is a title unto itself. I've worked with the best and the worst. I myself had an extremely successful run as a PT Manager for many years before going independent. I tried to do the job exactly how I would want it done if I were a trainer.

Walk The Talk

Several years ago I was training at a gym that hadn't hit its goals in months. Not enough memberships, smoothies, or personal training had been sold in a very long time. Even though a few of us were still very successful as individual trainers, overall morale was low and everyone there was miserable. Trainers were quitting in record numbers, and PT Managers were coming and going. Even the members noticed that none of these transient managers were good at their job. They felt the strange uneasiness in the air and were growing less and less comfortable in the gym.

For the fifth time in six months, we got a new PT Manager. This guy was different. He held a meeting the day he got there. First he introduced himself. Then he said this:

"My job is to help you make more money."

Now *that's* a bold statement! I had never before met a PTM who would dare make this claim. This guy viewed managing trainers like he was managing movie stars. His job was to do whatever was necessary to put us in front of the right people, get us the right gigs, and help us nail them. Like his predecessors, for him to get paid, we had to get paid. But unlike them, he realized that this goal could be reached more effectively by *valuing* rather than *exploiting* his staff. He worked for us as much as we worked for him, and it became a fun, goal-oriented team environment for the first time in ages.

He got up-to-date on the individual members and trainers, and sold lots of personal training. He hooked up the trainers who deserved it and mentored the trainers that needed it. This dude even fired the trainers who had it coming, making the staff stronger.

He made good on his bold statement and we all made more money.

The Other Side

Unfortunately, some PTMs do nothing to add to your paycheck. The worst of them will actually harm your business if you do not actively prevent it. It sounds counterintuitive but it's true. Not everything in the world makes sense.

PTMs have been known to undersell their own staff by offering lower rates or free sessions to clients who were already happy paying the normal rate. The trainer takes a pay cut every time this happens. (Ironically, in the long run, so does the PTM.) Worse still, they usually don't tell you first, meaning you go to train your client and it's for less than you negotiated. Not cool.

You have probably had this type of manager already as they exist in all businesses. These guys and gals expect their staff to work harder than they ever will, often asking for favors (early renewals) with nothing to offer in return (new clients.)

Don't assume your PTM can sell either. It's possible that your PTM is an inferior trainer and salesman to you. They are sometimes hired because the gym simply cannot find anyone better. When there is not a "best candidate" for a position, the *least worst* candidate prevails. Unfortunately, this is standard practice in every industry in the world. But that's okay; although having a great PTM can be a huge asset, a quality trainer will dominate with or without one. You must be able to handle your own sales and renewals regardless of whether your PT Manager is an angel or a demon.

Take The Lead

So what does the PTM actually do? In addition to paperwork, cold calls, scheduling first work-outs, recruiting, staffing, and developing trainers, the PTM *sells personal training*. I would argue that every single other task falls, either directly or indirectly, under the umbrella of sales (more in Chapter 12.) Whether it means getting a member excited about a future session, or giving a trainer the tools to administer world-class workouts and close their own deals, the PTM's job is always, ultimately to get more business for the club. That means more business for the trainers that deserve it. Any potential business your PTM (or anyone else) sends your way is called a lead.

Leads can come from anywhere. Although most of the time leads are new members, they can also be members prospected by the PTM himself, front desk inquiries, or former clients. When you are new, take every lead you can.

Some PTMs give leads out on a "first come/first served" basis, while others distribute them directly to trainers or hand them out at staff meetings. Most do a combination of these methods. Sometimes leads already have active (paying) sessions. As we've discussed, it's often referred to as "point-of-sale" when the lead/client already purchased sessions. A smart PTM will give the best leads to the top trainers. They will make it worthwhile for the PTM when it's time to close or renew.

Good Cop / Bad Cop

A good PTM is a valuable asset to have when it comes time for enforcing rates or charging for late cancellations. If your PTM has your back, he or she will make sure you don't get screwed in the situation that you show up for a 6am appointment but your client does not. A skilled and confident PTM can also play "bad cop" to your "good cop" when it comes time to raise the "entry level" rate your client has been paying for far too long.

In other words, with a qualified PTM, you do not have to be the one to tell your clients news they may not want to hear, like a rate increase or a charge for a late cancellation. The bad cop (your PTM) does that. As the good cop, it's out of your hands. You can say "Hey, this is coming straight from the top. If it was up to me…"

AS THE GOOD COP, IT'S OUT OF YOUR HANDS.

A SKILLED AND CONFIDENT PT MANAGER CAN PLAY "BAD COP" TO YOUR "GOOD COP."

A lesser PTM is incapable of playing good cop/bad cop and will kowtow to all client whims, even when they violate the PT agreement, common sense, or courtesy. These managers were probably too weak to enforce their own rates when (and if) they were ever trainers themselves. A good PTM always has the top trainers' backs, and will try to get you as much money as possible for your hard work.

Not Everything In Life Is Fair

You will hear colleagues talk about the PTM. "He was unfair. He played favorites!" Damn right. His favorites were probably the trainers that did their jobs and worked hard. "He didn't give me good leads," some say. That may very well be true. The trainer who wonders this must ask him or herself how much business they've brought to the table to deserve such leads. The motion picture *Glengarry Glen Ross* put it best: "Good leads are for closers." If you can't close a bad lead then don't expect a good one. Those leads are reserved for the trainers that bring value to the team. If you put in the effort and are punctual, you will be one of those trainers in time. Anyway, the best lead is the one in front of you so continue to prospect. Sell some business off the floor and you will get good leads if your PTM is not an idiot.

Client acquisition still rests on you. No matter what anybody says, obstacles can be overcome. No excuses. During the Great Recession of 2008, I was PTM at a wonderful, yet aggressive (in terms of sales) New York City health club with a monthly personal training goal in excess of $200,000. When every news outlet and media source advised cutting back on "luxuries such as personal training," my team still smashed records. We did exactly what this book says to do and those of us who were willing to earn it thrived despite any odds.

Accept it. Like many other things worth doing, no matter who your PTM is, you will have to put forth great effort to achieve results. Isn't that what you want to express to your clients anyway?

PT Manager As A Career

A lot of successful trainers transition well into becoming PT Managers. Others have no interest in it at all. Excelling at either requires great discipline and a strong work ethic so it's no surprise there is an overlap. Just remember, while being a trainer means being accountable for you and your clients only, being a PTM means being responsible for *every trainer* and *all of their clients!* I would not recommend trying to be a PTM without first having sustained long-term success as a personal trainer.

CHAPTER 7

INDEPENDENT'S DAY

> "ALWAYS BEAR IN MIND THAT YOUR OWN RESOLUTION TO SUCCEED IS MORE IMPORTANT THAN ANY ONE THING."
> —ABRAHAM LINCOLN

There may come a day when you decide the gym is not the place for you. Fear not, as there is a whole other world of career personal training out there: the world of independent training. Many (but not all) personal trainers ultimately want to work in this capacity. It is completely understandable for a trainer to eventually want to want to quit working for the man. Training privately means that you get to work for yourself (or more accurately, directly for your clients,) wear the clothes you want, and never have to attend a staff meeting again. Naturally, after doing the math, newly independent trainers and those considering it see how much more money they could potentially make with the gym out of the equation.

Not Always So

While it seems that you should take home double your paycheck without the gym taking its cut, in reality there are more costs to working for yourself than one may realize. First of all, you need a place to train. While it is ideal to train your clients in a place that costs you nothing, like their home or a public park, those scenarios do not work for everybody. Chances are that you will have to pay for some type of space to train at least a few of your clients.

Most gyms will not allow independent trainers to work on their premises. This is reasonable. It's mainly because if there is someone in the building who is willing to pay money for personal training, the gym wants to be the ones selling it. In 2007, I removed the pop band Coldplay and their trainer from my gym for this very reason. (Don't shed a tear for them; I'm sure they had the budget to rent a space.) In retrospect, I absolutely would have let them train there, if the trainer had just approached me like a man and asked. Instead, he acted like it was his house. The bottom line is, don't bring your clients into a gym that specifically prohibits independent training. It is a bitch move. Find a gym you can rent. Facilities may charge you by the client or by the hour. Some charge a flat monthly fee. Either way, it will cost you money. Personal trainer insurance will cost you too, and most establishments require it.

I am of the belief that time is our most valuable commodity. When you work as an independent personal trainer you spend a lot of time commuting. You may never build your business to a point where all your clients come to you in the same place. Most independent trainers I know work out of many locations and do a lot of running around. If you have thirty minutes between appointments and you work at a gym, you can enjoy a snack, get a quick workout, or take a shower. As an independent, if you need to be across town, you have to spend those thirty minutes hustling! It can wind up taking twice as many hours to do half as many sessions. All of the sudden, it doesn't look like double the paycheck anymore. There are no short cuts. Just like at the health clubs and high-end studios, you still have to work very hard and consistently.

The Legendary Tompkins Square Park

Not only is training outdoors invigorating, inspiring, and fun, it also saves you some overhead expenses. Parks and playgrounds are quickly becoming the preferred gyms for personal training. Why work out under fluorescent lights when we can train beneath the sun instead?

You Can't Take It With You

The real tricky part about working for yourself is getting clients. Often when personal trainers leave a gym to go independent, they try to take the gym's clients with them. Notice I said "the gym's clients" not "their clients." I understand this is confusing. Allow me to clarify.

When you work directly for a gym, then technically, all training is done through the gym, and not directly from you. Gyms go out of their way to make this clear to the members. PT registration forms always state somewhere that sessions are purchased from the organization, not the trainer. The gym does this so that in the event that your employment ends, clients know up front that they will be assigned a new trainer. You can't blame the gym; their job is to make money.

There is also something called a Non-Competition agreement that trainers sign when they start working for almost any commercial gym. It says that they won't solicit clients that they met through said gym. If you signed one, then keep your word. Obviously they're not going to call the cops if you try to take their business but stealing clients is like school on a Saturday... no class. While not an overtly cowardly move like training off-the-books in someone else's gym, it's still beneath us. Also, your clients may be less loyal to you than you think. They are often more loyal to their comfort zone, the gym. You'd be surprised at how your best client may prioritize the location over the trainer.

The fitness industry is a small world. Sometimes your reputation is all you have, and it's nice to be known as a class act. It's a big "fuck you" to your (former) employers if you choose to steal from them. Leave the gym's clients where you found them. If any of them want to train with you bad enough, they will seek you out on their own in time. Besides that, it's an unfortunate fact that many independent trainers return to a gym within six months. You don't want to embarrass yourself if you ever need a reference. So what to do? Like we said in the beginning of this book, you need a steady flow of new business to survive in this industry.

New Business, First Workouts, And Referrals

If prospecting is king for the big box trainers, and point-of-sale is your main opportunity at the boutique, then referrals surely rule the proverbial playground for the independents. Because you work for yourself, your only real opportunity to prospect is at random everyday places, where meeting your next client is pretty unlikely. Every single personal trainer I've ever met in my life has been approached at a party or social gathering and been asked repeatedly by strangers and acquaintances: "How do I get 6-pack abs?" or "How do I get bigger?" Chances are these kind folks will not train with you. Don't waste your time. Yes, prospecting in parks (that's where I met my #1 client ever) or other places where people actually exercise is possible, but the opportunities are few and far between. Obviously, point-of-sale doesn't exist because there is no PT manager, studio owner, or sales rep to sell for you. However, because your private clients should by now be sold on you, not a specific gym or fitness fad, referrals will take on a whole new life.

Usually, referred clients are practically sold by the time they contact you. In this case, conducting the first workout is like grilling a fine porterhouse steak: your job is to simply not fuck it up. You are dealing with a different type of buyer. You must still create a sense of urgency in the prospective client, but not quite as much as you do at the clubs. You have fewer leads from which to draw as an independent, so owning your first workouts becomes even more important.

The prospective client in the big box gym is generally someone who, in looking for a recognizable brand, is susceptible to advertising and sales tactics. Most of the time, they do not know what they want. When you work for such a gym, use these traits to your advantage. Conversely, the clients in the boutiques are what are known as "self-actualized buyers." They want (what they think is) the best and they are willing to pay for it. Once again, use it to your advantage when you can. You have a different type of lead as a private trainer. These clients generally go with their own eyes and the experience of others they know and trust. Chances are that they know someone who has gotten desirable results while training with you, and decided to go right to the source rather than consult a search engine. Good for them.

I can tell you with utmost honesty, as a trainer with a relatively high online profile, that at least 90% of my business is based on word-of-mouth alone. That's right; very few people who are serious about training contact me online. At the time of this writing, I have only one consistent client who "met" me on the internet. While it is possible that group discount websites can get you clients, they are often not serious, and usually reach out only to cash in on a perceived bargain. They may never even show up to claim that Groupon. I've had luck with direct mailers in the past, though it is costlier than other methods.

I absolutely encourage you to pursue all avenues of client acquisition, but it's my experience that simply asking your clients for referrals (even throwing them an extra session on you for each paying referred client) is much more efficient and effective than many of the other more timely ventures.

Postcards From The Edge

When I first went into independent business I printed thousands of these postcards. I went to www.USPS.com and got the apartment numbers of many upscale residential buildings with in-house fitness centers. Then I did direct mailers just like the big clubs do. It worked. I got a minimum of one client from every single building I sent my postcards to. Each mailing paid for itself within a session or two, and most of these clients remained with me long after my expenses recouped. I also kept a stack of these at the coffee shop across the street from Tompkins Square Park, which I continue to do to this day.

The Theory Of Natural Selection And Your PT clients

When I began as a personal trainer, I took all comers. I trained clients I did not relate to and sometimes didn't even like. I suggested exercises that, looking back, were not the ones I would have chosen today. Once, I even administered a workout simply because my client read about it in an article clearly written by someone who never trained anybody. At the dawn of my career, I tried to be everything to everyone. All types of client relations spawned in the primordial ooze of my early days, but many did not to survive. That's Darwin, darlin'. Over time, the inappropriate weed themselves out. But in the beginning, you really need to take them all. Your client base will get better the longer you train. Hopefully, by the time you go fully independent, you already have at least one or two clients, but it's okay if you don't. I literally had zero. Be ready work your ass off. More than ever, you are the only one accountable for you.

I am grateful to say that these days, I truly like all of my clients. It is not because I'm a great trainer. It's simply because I've been doing it long enough.

The Tax Man Cometh

Benjamin Franklin famously remarked that "nothing can be said to be certain, except death and taxes." Personal trainers should listen. We sometimes make a lot of money in cash. It is important that we claim some or all of it. I am by no means a tax expert, but I know we must account for our living. Find out from a professional what you can deduct and do it. If you ignore the IRS they will not go away. They may in fact come back to haunt you.

"OUR CONSTITUTION IS ESTABLISHED... BUT IN THIS WORLD, NOTHING CAN BE SAID TO BE CERTAIN, EXCEPT DEATH AND TAXES." —*BEN FRANKLIN.*

I also recommend talking to a professional in your area regarding incorporation or starting a limited liability company, as these matters differ from state to state. It may or may not be the best move for your business. Simply being "self employed," though less glamorous, may be more cost efficient.

A Man Of Many Hats

I've lived a lot of life and seen a lot of sights. In addition to some former vocations mentioned in the first chapter (low-budget rock star and spring-break emcee), I've also been an exterminator, a parade marshal, and even a clown. I've travelled the world and met all kinds of people. I have many stories to tell and they're all true.

ONLY TWO OF THESE PARADE MARSHALS WERE IN THE 1939 CLASSIC *"THE WIZARD OF OZ."*

I can honestly say that working in personal training is the best job I've ever had. It's a dream job. If you are fortunate enough to earn a successful independent career for yourself, never lose sight of how special that is.

I WAS NEVER AS GOOD AT CLOWNING AS THIS MAN, BUFFO THE WORLD'S STRONGEST CLOWN, A TOP-NOTCH ENTERTAINER WHO IS JUST AS COMFORTABLE DOING A STRONGMAN SHOW AS HE IS PERFORMING MAGIC TRICKS FOR CHILDREN.

CHAPTER 8

THE TRAINER EXPERIENCE

"TELL ME AND I'LL FORGET.
SHOW ME, I MAY REMEMBER.
INVOLVE ME AND I'LL UNDERSTAND."
-CONFUCIUS

lthough we will not be discussing specific programming in this volume, the actual service we sell is still a workout. As we know, there is a lot more to conducting an amazing workout than the individual exercises involved. In reality, they rank behind many other factors. Let's discuss those factors.

I would once again like to point out that the way we train our clients is not necessarily the same way we train ourselves. Our job is (1) to make sure that the client gets a workout he or she cannot do without us and (2) to build a relationship. This includes motivating, inspiring, and guiding them through the journey. That's the trainer experience!

The following, while not technically "working out," are arguably even more important:

Physical And Verbal Involvement

When your client shows up to train they should be greeted with a smile and a handshake. Look them in the eye. I have seen trainers instantly overcome by a look of disgust the moment that they realize that their client arrived, and they must now stop watching TV or eating. Not good. Remember, although exercise is your job, and you may observe hundreds of push-ups a day, your

client has been looking forward to these push-ups all week, and is paying you to be there. If someone chooses to show up to an appointment where they will be exchanging their hard-earned money for your time, then make them feel good about that decision. This is the essence of building good relationships. The most successful trainers are the ones whose clients look forward to seeing them. Imagine that the workout is the best hour of your client's day. Show them you care! Be present. The physical and verbal involvement begins the second you two make eye contact, and lasts, uninterrupted, until you part ways.

SHOW THEM YOU CARE! BE PRESENT.

IT'S A GOOD IDEA TO ACTUALLY PUT YOUR HAND BETWEEN THE SHOULDER BLADES AND SAY "SQUEEZE WHERE YOU FEEL MY HAND."

WHEN HANDING WEIGHTS TO YOUR CLIENT,
USE A "PINCHED GRIP" WHENEVER POSSIBLE.

When showing a client an exercise or posture during a session, physically cue them. In addition to saying "Squeeze your shoulder blades back," I believe it is a good idea to actually put your hand between the shoulder blades and say "squeeze where you feel my hand." Remember to always get your client's permission before touching them for any reason.

Do not demonstrate an exercise unless it is absolutely necessary. You are better off guiding the client through it than demonstrating. When you simply show them an exercise they will miss out on the subtlety of how it feels. Additionally, clients generally do not enjoy when a trainer makes something they are struggling with look easy. Be there for them, not you.

Worse than demonstrating a few reps, of course, is using your client's session to show off or work out. This happens more often than you can imagine. The trainer demonstrates a pull-up, and all of the sudden, he's on his tenth rep, while the client stands there embarrassed, emasculated, and confused. Work out on your time, not your clients'. It pains me every single time I see this happen.

WRAP YOUR
CLIENTS' HANDS
FOR THEM.

Another great way to be physically involved is to hand the weights or other equipment to your client when training them. It's a part of the service that we provide. Don't let your ego get in the way. Pick up the dumbbells and gently hand them over. If I go to 5-Star restaurant (or even a crappy restaurant) I expect that the waiter will bring me my food because it's part of the service I'm paying for. I do not expect the waiter to think he's too good to do so, or to feel comfortable enough with me that he thinks he no longer has to. The same is true with people who pay for your service. Hand them the weights. Use "pinch grip" when possible. This makes it easier for them to take the weights out of your hand. For that matter, wrap your clients' hands for them when doing a boxing session. Help them with their gloves and be as involved as possible.

THIS IS HOW YOU HELP YOUR CLIENT UP.

When counting reps out loud, I find that backwards is usually preferable to forward. When you're counting "eleven... twelve... thirteen," the set can feel like it will go on forever. But when clients hear "three... two... one," they know exactly what's happening. Counting backwards allows them to see the end is coming and pace themselves. It motivates them. Always be affirmative and encouraging with your words and body language. A "Hell Yeah" and a high-five go a long way!

Progressive Flow

The warm-up is your chance to talk and feel your client out. I train a gentleman who is a high end art dealer. His work is known around the world and he has a lot more celebrity clients than I do! This guy can (and has) trained with many of the biggest names in personal training. He likes training with me best because I always start the workout by asking how he's feeling. He actually told me that. He appreciates that I like to see where he's at and then see where the workout takes us. Never forget the importance of open-ended questions, no matter how long a client has been with you. If his back hurts we start with stretching. If he ran across town to the session and is all fired up and ready to rock, then we get right to the tough stuff. If he's half-asleep, we warm up and ease into it.

Be in the moment. Don't worry about the next exercise or even the next rep. Stay focused on exactly what's in front of you. The ability to flow organically through a workout, while riding the physical and emotional highs and lows of the client, is one of the hardest things to put your finger on. It involves attention, intuition, and feel. Don't follow a workout you're reading off a clipboard or an iPad; follow what your client is experiencing. Live in the present.

BE IN THE MOMENT.
DON'T WORRY ABOUT THE NEXT EXERCISE OR EVEN THE NEXT REP.
STAY FOCUSED ON EXACTLY WHAT'S IN FRONT OF YOU.

Shine The Spotlight

The workout, the session, the relationship, and the experience are really all about your client. It has frequently been said that you should try to imagine a spotlight beaming down on the person you're training. Shine bright, baby! It's their session, not yours. The focus stays on them and so does the conversation. Even if they feign interest, most of your clients don't care how much sleep you got last night or which gym patrons you find attractive.

Stay physically close to your client too. Never put a trainee on a treadmill and walk away. If you feel that you absolutely must put your client on a large piece of equipment that doesn't require a trainer, at least keep them company.

DO NOT PUT A CLIENT ON A TREADMILL AND WALK AWAY. IT MAY BE BEST TO AVOID THE TREADMILL ALTOGETHER AS IT IS OFTEN NOT THE BEST WAY TO USE THE GYM, AS THIS PHOTO ILLUSTRATES.

A Word About Niche Training

Many of us have a niche in our own personal workouts. Power lifting, MMA, and calisthenics can each be considered a niche. We do what we like to do, as we all should in life. If you are a football player, it makes sense that some of your own workouts would be sport-specific. If you are passionate about the pull-up bar, then naturally your workouts will include a lot of bar-work.

But niche training does not always pay the bills. A friend of mine who is a world-famous trainer of athletes and nationally ranked body builders once told me that he trains competitors because it's his passion. He trains doctors and lawyers because it's his job. But they all get 100% attention.

You may be surprised to see trainers who are known for one style, sometimes doing exercises with their clients that defy what you'd expect. Likely, this is because the trainer is a pro, and realizes that their job is to give a workout appropriate for the trainee in front of them, with the equipment in front of them, rather than adhere to preconceived notions.

ALL THE BEST TRAINERS USE THE EQUIPMENT IN FRONT OF THEM TO DO WHAT'S BEST FOR THE CLIENT IN FRONT OF THEM, REGARDLESS OF IF IT'S THEIR NICHE OR NOT.

To be successful professional personal trainers, we need to make sure that our clients want to work with us. Giving appropriate workouts comes right after showing up on time and being enjoyable to be around, in terms of being successful. This usually means sticking to the basics. Don't worry about showing off your "style" with every move. If you're the "Resistance Band Guy" (which I once heard a trainer refer to himself as) please refrain from incorporating resistance bands into every exercise with each client just for the hell of it. I certainly have my favorite personal moves, but if they're not right for the client, the moves stay with me.   Keep it simple. Ernest Hemmingway once remarked: "What amateurs call a style is usually only the unavoidable awkwardness in first trying."

Standing Tall

It is generally not a good policy to sit while your client is working out. First of all, it looks bad. When a trainee is busting their ass, pouring their heart out, sweating and bleeding from the soul, the trainer who is sitting slumped over on a plyo-box, looking at his phone, does a good job only at exposing himself as a fraud.

As far as safety goes, many people hire trainers to make sure they are lifting properly and are being spotted attentively. This service is impossible to provide if you're sitting around in the background. You have to be standing right there with your clients when they're performing those overhead presses, in close proximity and physically present. Remember what we said at the beginning of the chapter: Physical and verbal involvement should last the whole workout.

PHYSICAL AND VERBAL INVOLVEMENT SHOULD LAST THE WHOLE WORKOUT.

Even when your client is doing floor exercises, sitting is a bad policy. Yes, you need to be available to them and in their physical space, even when they're on the ground, but this can be easily accomplished from a kneeling position, which comes off as more professional.

Your clients really shouldn't be sitting either. Chances are they've been sitting all day. Unless he or she has a specific injury or issue that prohibits them from standing, try to keep your client on their feet. It sometimes surprises me when I see trainees who have been sitting hunched over a desk for ten hours at their job, show up at the gym only to be put in a machine that compresses them even more. This workout may be the only chance your client gets to stand on their own two feet all day long. Grant it to them.

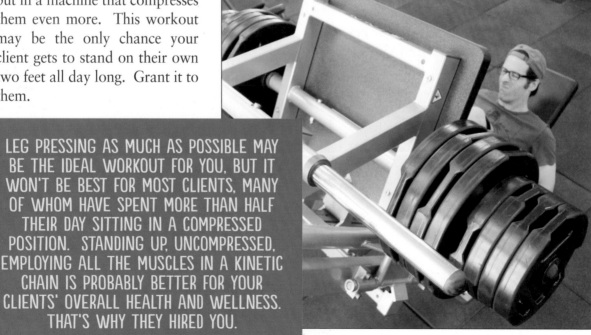

LEG PRESSING AS MUCH AS POSSIBLE MAY BE THE IDEAL WORKOUT FOR YOU, BUT IT WON'T BE BEST FOR MOST CLIENTS, MANY OF WHOM HAVE SPENT MORE THAN HALF THEIR DAY SITTING IN A COMPRESSED POSITION. STANDING UP, UNCOMPRESSED, EMPLOYING ALL THE MUSCLES IN A KINETIC CHAIN IS PROBABLY BETTER FOR YOUR CLIENTS' OVERALL HEALTH AND WELLNESS. THAT'S WHY THEY HIRED YOU.

THE ABILITY TO SEE THINGS FROM A DIFFERENT PERSPECTIVE IS A HELPFUL SKILL FOR PERSONAL TRAINERS.

Client Expectations

When discussing how to give fantastic workouts that keep our clients coming back, we must first ask ourselves what it is that the client expects in the first place. Try to see things from their perspective. And while we as trainers know that making the workout enjoyable, fun, and engaging, is probably the most important part of a session, the client doesn't. This beckons the question, what exactly do they want from the workout? The answer is not big muscles, lower body fat, or to get laid more often. Sure they hope for those things over time, but nobody really believes that those goals can be achieved from only one session. Even your most misinformed, gullible prospect knows that's impossible. If they don't, it's your job to set them straight.

There are generally more immediate expectations from the workout. Here are the main three:

1. Accelerated Heart Rate

It is reasonable for anyone undertaking a personal training session to expect that their heart will beat harder and faster than usual. Most of your clients are inactive for most of the day. If they take the time out of their busy day to book a workout with their trainer, they deserve for you to make their heart beat. Even if you're not doing a cardio workout, I still believe that, at least for some of the session, you need to treat your trainee to that heart-against-the-ribcage feel. Most people will not do this on their own. They need you. And they will walk out of the gym feeling like they truly accomplished something by training with you. They will be right.

2. Sweat

If you are new to the fitness business, it may strike you as odd that I need to mention this at all. "It's a workout," you may think. "*Of course*, you'll sweat!"

However this is not always the case. I have observed countless personal training sessions where the seated individual being trained never even exerts hard enough to break a sweat. For shame. Not every client needs to be reduced to a wet, sopping mess, but for heaven's sake, they gotta perspire!

3. Muscular Exertion and Soreness

One should also expect to experience some feeling in their muscles during a workout, not to mention a degree of subsequent soreness. While it is a fact that over time, muscles get more resilient to particular exercises and training methods, there is no excuse for the trainee not to feel some type of exertion and soreness somewhere in the body.

Like we said in the second chapter of this book, part of your job is to give your client a workout that they cannot do without you. Well, another is to help them get results. Meeting this expectation helps drastically with both. Mind you, sore does not mean injured! A good rule of thumb is that if it's a dull pain then it's a by-product of exercise. Any sharp, shooting pain, however, may demand medical attention. Train hard and smart.

There are exceptions to everything. This list may not be appropriate for elderly, sick, or injured clients. Consult your client's physician if you have any doubts about their health. That said, there is no reason that any able-bodied trainee should not experience all three of these expectations every single time.

> PART OF YOUR JOB IS TO GIVE YOUR CLIENT A WORKOUT THAT THEY CANNOT DO WITHOUT YOU. ANOTHER IS TO HELP THEM GET RESULTS.

Okay, Okay... A Little About Exercise

The body moves the way the body moves. You can curl a dumbbell or straight bar, hammer grip or traditional, but a curl will always be bicep flexion. It will always be a curl. Just as a squat will always be a squat, in spite of its limitless variations. We cannot change our anatomy or its intrinsic movement patterns. But, still, we do not want our training to grow stagnant.

Session after session, week after week, and hopefully year after year, we will train the same person in these same basic human movement patterns. When I refer to "modality" or "mode" I mean the medium in which we choose to train: the difference between, say, a full body barbell workout at the squat cage, and an equally-intense and effective workout where we use nothing more than the client's own bodyweight for resistance. Without getting exercise-specific, I would like to address the importance of being able to switch modes from one workout to another, or even within the same workout. This will help you be a successful trainer for many reasons.

For one, mixing things up will keep your client from getting bored. The value of this cannot be overstated. Your client is probably coming to you after one or more failed attempts to get fit without you. Why couldn't they do it on their own or even with a different trainer? Whether it's because they didn't get results, or just got bored, something caused them to lose interest along the way.

As trainers and fitness enthusiasts, we have all had highs and lows in our own training. We hit walls in our progress from time to time. We often make a big deal about getting past physical plateaus, while failing to recognize that mental ones can be just as stifling. As a trainer, changing the modalities by which we train our clients is essential for avoiding and overcoming both plateaus.

Again I'd like to say that the movement patterns of the human body will remain the same until evolution changes us, and we simply don't have time for that! Being comfortable in several basic modalities is one of the best ways for us to adapt change and keep it fun. I'm not talking about doing Jiu-Jitsu, Pilates, body-building, and gymnastics in the same session, or even with the same client. I am simply saying that almost any personal training workout can be done in a fashion to include barbells, dumbbells, sandbags, stability balls, or whatever equipment is on hand (which may be none at all.)

One should be able to train in any environment too. All professional personal trainers benefit from knowing how to work in small spaces, particularly during peak hours. Use what is around you, and co-exist peacefully with whatever other trainers or members are in the vicinity. Adaptation is key to being effective in any gym, studio, playground, or even living room for that matter.

ONE SHOULD BE ABLE TO TRAIN IN ANY ENVIRONMENT.

One more thing: I know it can be fun to incorporate toys like bands, boards, bells, and whistles. It seems that a new product or fad comes along every day. Just be aware that, while these pieces of equipment are not always bad, the overwhelming majority of them, while novel, are unnecessary. Don't become dependent or overestimate their value. Any trainer worth his salt needs no more equipment than something to pick up, something to hang from, and something to step up on, if anything at all. Use props to go with the flow and get the most out of your surroundings, but always remember it's about the workout and the relationship, not any individual piece of equipment—they can always be substituted, even eliminated.

ANY TRAINER WORTH HIS SALT NEEDS NO MORE EQUIPMENT THAN SOMETHING TO PICK UP, SOMETHING TO HANG FROM, AND SOMETHING TO STEP UP ON, IF ANYTHING AT ALL.

More Done In Less Time

Your ability to be efficient is part of why you were hired. Chances are that your clients do not like to work out (at least not yet.) Helping them get it done in a timely and effective manner is one of your greatest attributes as a trainer. Be the expert.

Before we talk about how to get more done in less time, let's revisit our list of client expectations. They are accelerated heart rate, sweat, and muscular soreness. Here are some time tested ways of going about it:

Super-setting upper and lower body movements (push-ups into squats or shoulder presses into deadlifts, for example) is a sure-fire way of smashing your clients workout expectations, keeping the relationship alive and your paycheck steady. So is super-setting exercises that alternate between opposing muscle groups (push-ups into pull-ups, planks into bridgework, curls into dips, etc.) These methods both work along the principal of "active recovery" which means that while one muscle, muscle group, or part of the body is resting, we train a different one to maximize our time and performance. Circuit training does this too.

Circuit training is a work out in which we move the trainee from one exercise to another with little to no rest in between. Circuits can be body part specific (for example, military presses, lateral raises, rear deltoid flies, repeat for shoulders) or incorporate numerous muscle groups (squats, kettlebell swings, push-ups, pull-ups, dips, repeat for full body.) These are excellent ways to train, however no circuit is appropriate until the client knows how to do every exercise involved first. (See Appendix B for sample routines.)

Other methods of maximizing strength, cardio, and conditioning efficiently include plyometrics (explosive or airborne movements such as jump squats or clapping pushups,) interval training (time on/time off,) and compound movements (clean and press, for example.)

EXAMPLES OF PLYOMETRIC EXERCISES.

The Experience Of Others Around You

It's good practice to look out for the general well being of the people around you. There are sure to be other trainers, gym members, and staff in your general vicinity and making friends is a better policy than making enemies. Be polite, courteous, and respectful.

Rule number one of gym etiquette is Clean Up Your Mess. I recommend doing this as you train. It's very simple. After you use a piece of equipment, put it back where it belongs. If you place weights onto a bench or piece of equipment, then remove them when you're done. It takes almost no time when you put your stuff away as you go.

If other members need to share equipment, then invite them to work in with you whenever possible. Being a personal trainer does not entitle you to monopolize any part of the gym. The fact that your client is paying you means nothing to the guy waiting for the squat rack. Act like a fitness professional at all times and share the gym. Your client will respect you more for it.

It's also a good idea to refrain from speaking negatively about other trainers, exercises, gym patrons, or *anything* else, for that matter. Go back to the childhood rule: If you don't have something nice to say, then don't say anything at all. This is particularly true when it comes to different methods of training. I've heard everybody talk shit about everyone else's modality and it's never a turn-on. In reality, calisthenics, weight training, running, and yoga are all great ways to get in shape. A list of effective ways to train would go on endlessly. Be in the habit of encouraging your clients by spreading positivity, not talking trash. No one loves a hater.

Treat others as you would like to be treated. Try not to yell, scream, or curse too loudly on the training floor. Be aware of who is around you. That's all I got to say about that.

IT DOESN'T MATTER HOW LONG YOU'VE BEEN TRAINING. RULE #1 OF GYM ETIQUETTE IS CLEAN UP YOUR MESS.

Client Retention

I once attended a personal training workshop conducted by my boss at the time. It was a basic, run-of-the mill overview; everything he said was your standard PT banter—"assess your client, give a dynamic warm-up, begin the workout, blah, blah, blah." Nothing really stuck out to me. That is until I heard the following:

"Sometimes when I stop by the gym to observe you guys, I notice some trainers giving their clients a very solid workout. That makes me happy. Other times, I observe trainers just talking and laughing with their clients, not working out at all. That makes me even happier. The second client is guaranteed to renew."

Now, I cannot say that I agree with this gentleman entirely, but I do see his point. It comes down to the relationship. I am in the results business, but no matter what kind of spectacular results I help my clients achieve, my employment will end if the relationship is not there. Get them results, but make them smile too.

Some degree of client attrition is unavoidable, so don't beat yourself up when you lose a few along the way. But assuming that your whole entire client base doesn't skip town, *why shouldn't you keep training them?* It's up to you.

IT COMES DOWN TO THE RELATIONSHIP.

CHAPTER 9

TOP TEN DO'S

> "90% OF SUCCESS IS SHOWING UP."
> —WOODY ALLEN

here are certain habits that I believe can make or break a personal training career. Here are my top ten. I thought long and hard about which ones to include on this list. These are the ones that made the grade.

1. DO be on time.

This applies to everything in life. Showing up late is a sign of disrespect to your personal training client, or to whoever is waiting for you. There is no excuse for it. If you know it takes you thirty minutes to get to work then allow yourself forty-five. Being even five minutes late to anything simply means that you do not care enough to leave on time. It sends an "I don't give a shit about you" message loud and clear.

As a PT Manager, I could easily talk my way out of ever having to give a customer a refund, no matter what the reason. Even if the personal trainers I employed were at fault, I had a knack for keeping the clients' money when they were clearly in the right. I am not proud of this, but it's part of what I was hired to do. (See "Do Your Job" section of Chapter 4.) However, if a trainer showed up chronically late for a client, I replaced him. If the client wasn't satisfied, then and only then would I refund their money in full, no questions asked. Back in the day, I wouldn't even give a refund if a client got injured! But I had to for trainer lateness. It's too damn insulting and there's no excuse for it.

SHOWING UP LATE IS A SIGN OF DISRESPECT TO YOUR PERSONAL TRAINING CLIENT, OR TO WHOEVER IS WAITING FOR YOU.

2. DO call people when you say you will call them.

This one sounds easy, right? Well it is. If you tell a client (or potential client) that you'll check in with them the next day, then do it. Making a follow-up call can and will help you get business. If you tell someone that you will call to schedule an appointment, email them information, or find out the nearest sneaker store, then do it.

If you have absolutely no intention of calling a prospect (which should almost never be the case) then refrain from telling them that you will. It all comes down to follow-through. If you say you will do something, then you have to do it. Period.

3. DO look at your client.

Keep your eyes on the person you're training, not the TV, the attractive new member, or the clock. Obviously there is a safety element here in terms of enforcing proper form and spotting heavy weight when necessary, but there is a lot more too. Since the relationship with your client is at least as important for your business as the workout itself, looking at your client improves your paycheck, not just their safety. Maintaining eye contact is also very important. It not only shows concern, but respect. Always treat your client like a human being.

4. DO show up clean and smelling like soap and toothpaste.

A trainer who used to work for me would, every now and again, show up to his appointments smelling of Hennessy. And despite what he thought, the single splash of cheap, locker room cologne applied seconds before the session did nothing to mask it.

Has anyone ever seen a trainer, or gym manager, or front desk staff member eating McDonalds? I have about five hundred times. Even worse, I've smelled it. Smelling like this stuff is not only disgusting but incredibly unprofessional. If you absolutely must eat food heavily perfumed in chemically-concocted flavors, please do so off the gym floor. Wash your hands and brush your teeth before training.

The same is true for cigarettes. If for some reason, you must smoke, you should probably take a shower before you train anybody. Allow yourself ample time to do so. Like eating fast food, it goes without saying that this habit sets a bad example.

Healthy things are not necessarily better. You don't want to smell like broccoli, boiled egg, or protein-powder farts during a session either. I travel with deodorant, floss, toothbrush and toothpaste at all times. Hand sanitizer too. Although soap is better, it's not always around. If that's a bit much for you, then at least keep some breath mints in your pocket.

5. DO make sure your client is being challenged.

If you have an uninjured 200 lb. man doing overhead presses with 4 lb. dumbbells, then he is not being challenged. Neither is the lady sitting on a Swiss ball, doing nothing else. Don't kid yourself or your clients. Make sure they're being challenged for at least part of your time together.

While it's true that some people just don't want to work very hard, we as trainers owe them some kind of push, at the very least. Select appropriate exercises and resistance. You can give plenty of breaks if that's what is required. Just don't waste their time.

THIS MAN IS NOT WORKING HARD ENOUGH.

THAT'S MORE LIKE IT!

6. DO be nice to your clients (Abusive Trainers)

A colleague of mine recently overheard the following comment while waiting in line at the grocery store: "I can't believe my trainer is so mean to me! I'm paying him! He should at least be nice to me."

After all these years it still amazes me when I see personal trainers behaving in overtly hostile ways to their clients. I don't just mean disrespecting them by showing up late; I am referring to insults, jabs, condescending comments, and overall negativity. Yes I am the first to admit that some trainer/client relationships have dominant/submissive tones. Any time you're standing over some one, telling them what to do, and they listen, perhaps there is some level of dominance at play. But unlike the boss at their job, where your clients must work to earn a living, you were chosen. They are paying you to tell them what to do.

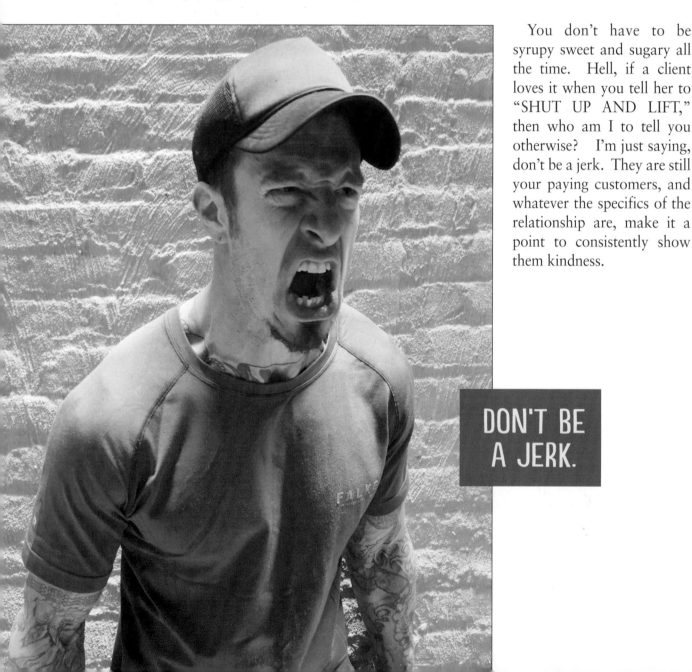

You don't have to be syrupy sweet and sugary all the time. Hell, if a client loves it when you tell her to "SHUT UP AND LIFT," then who am I to tell you otherwise? I'm just saying, don't be a jerk. They are still your paying customers, and whatever the specifics of the relationship are, make it a point to consistently show them kindness.

DON'T BE A JERK.

6. DO make sure men train their lower bodies and women train their upper bodies.

Fellas: First of all, you're not strong if you don't have strong legs. Period. I could end the male portion of this section right here but there is a bit more to say.

There are many reasons to train legs. Barring injuries or disabilities, there are zero reasons not to. Men often do not want to train their legs because they are only concerned with a nice looking upper body. They want to lose their belly, have 6-pack abs, big biceps, and broad shoulders. I understand that. But what they don't understand is that training your legs helps with that. Because the legs contain the largest muscle-groups in the body, training them promotes natural muscle building activity in the body. This helps the entire body get leaner and more muscular.

All those gym rats who want to lose their guts need to cut down on the crunches and start doing squats, lunges, and deadlifts. Big, compound leg movements recruit multiple large muscle groups as well as the abdominals. They expend more energy and burn more calories than almost any other type of exercise. Building strong legs will raise your client's metabolism all day every day. As long as they don't start eating more, they will get leaner and leaner.

Just as it is imperative for your male clients to train their legs, your female clients will benefit immensely from training their arms, shoulders, back, and chest. I have personally had female clients from age seventeen to fifty progress and perfect their first pushups and pull-ups, even if they were hesitant at the beginning. They may hire you because they want to sculpt and tone their thighs, claves, and butt, but what they don't know is that incorporating upper body will make them leaner and more toned overall. All their clothes will fit them better. I have seen women who *thought* they didn't want to train their arms fall in love with upper body training. They look and feel infinitely better because of it!

8. DO encourage your clients to try things on their own.

If someone really wants to get in shape, I recommend that they exercise to varying degrees at least four days a week. Now, I don't care who you are, how many celebrities you train, what you charge, or how many sessions you do; a client who works with a trainer more than three days a week is *extremely* rare for anybody. Most personal training clients, even the most consistent ones, work with their trainer about once or twice a week, with intermittent weeks off throughout the year. Therefore, if they want results, they have to exercise without you.

It blows my mind when I see (presumably insecure) trainers actually discourage their clients from exercising. They are probably the same people who get easily threatened if their girlfriend or boyfriend speaks to a member of the opposite sex. Don't be that person. Perhaps they are afraid that their client will prefer a spin class or yoga lesson to their own services. This makes no sense. If your clients like the class, they will be glad you encouraged them to do it. When they achieve better results from the added workout, they will have you to thank for it. And suppose they do try something new and decide never to train with you again? So be it. At least you helped them find a mode of exercise that they enjoy. Maybe you weren't right for each other anyway. It's a cold, hard fact of life that not every trainer is a perfect fit for every client. Sometimes you're just not the right one. If this is ever the case, be cool about it.

IF THEY WANT RESULTS, THEY HAVE TO EXERCISE WITHOUT YOU.

The vast majority of the time, encouraging your client to run, bike, jog, or join a volleyball league will improve your client's health and make fitness a bigger part of their lives. It will also strengthen their relationship with you, the trainer, and produce greater results.

9. DO be certain your client is capable of doing what you ask.

Before your trainees can perform an overhead barbell squat, they must first be able to perform a body-weight squat. Before performing a body-weight squat, they have to be able to stand up and sit down with proper mechanics. And before that, we must make sure they can stand up straight. For real.

All too often, because trainers get bored, they put clients through exercises and drills seemingly just for the hell of it. You may love the overhead squat, but it may not be the right move for your client. If it is, then by all means do it; just make sure that your client is capable first. By the same token, if your client can't perform a proper push-up on the ground, don't have them do it on a pair of medicine balls just because you saw a fighter do it on the TV.

Heavy barbell squats or deadlifts without knowledge of form is a problem 100% of the time. Telling an obese man to do ten pull-ups doesn't help anybody, especially if he's incapable of doing one. It's embarrassing for the trainer, the client, and everyone in the gym. Train the person in front of you, not a hypothetical conception of who you thought he or she might be.

IF YOUR CLIENT CAN'T PERFORM A PROPER PUSH-UP ON THE GROUND, DON'T HAVE THEM DO IT ON A PAIR OF MEDICINE BALLS JUST BECAUSE YOU SAW A FIGHTER DO IT ON THE TV.

10. DO reach out to clients you haven't seen in a while.

A well-timed phone call can be critical in getting back one or two clients who may have dropped off along the way. Many times, clients are looking to come back and train but are too nervous to reach out. Remember, part of your job is to be a motivator, so try to get them back in the gym! For obvious reasons, good times to contact dormant clients include the day after Thanksgiving and New Years. Chances are they'll be thinking of returning anyway at these times. Keep the conversation open ended like "Hey I haven't seen you in a while. Everything ok?" not "Yo, let's book a session."

CHAPTER 10

TOP TEN DON'T'S

"DON'T DO WHAT DONNIE DON'T DOES."
-FROM "THE SIMPSONS"

hese are included as blatant examples of behavior that we as personal trainers (and future personal trainers) should avoid at all costs. Some of these bonehead moves not only put your client (and income) in potential jeopardy, but they really hurt personal training in general. Having one trainer on the floor who looks like an amateur makes everyone look bad. Acting like a professional requires showing respect to your clients, your fellow trainers, and yourself.

1. DON'T text message, talk on the phone, or play "Words with Friends" during a personal training session.

Non-personal trainers may look at this rule and wonder why it must be included. But unfortunately anyone who has spent a lot of time in a gym knows better. It is impossible to ignore the fact that many trainers spend more time looking at their mobile communication devices than they do at their clients. It happens all the time.

These activities are rude to engage in during many situations, even when not in a session. I wouldn't recommend texting while having a meal or conversation with someone either. But at least your dinner date isn't paying for your undivided attention. Your client is. What if you went to a dentist and he was texting during your root canal, even if he thought you weren't looking? I believe that placing a client on a lat pull-down machine, walking behind them, and sending an email is equally reprehensible.

WHAT IF YOU WENT TO A DENTIST AND HE WAS TEXTING DURING YOUR ROOT CANAL, EVEN IF HE THOUGHT YOU WEREN'T LOOKING?

2. DON'T eat while on the training floor.

Many personal trainers are on their feet for long periods of time. In an unrelated fact, many personal trainers eat frequently throughout the day. Yet I just said not to eat while on the training floor. This can prove to be quite a quagmire. We need to get our precious nutrients and still manage to work all day, don't we? Well, here's one time when we as professionals must simply suck it up. It's really not a big deal to go a few hours without eating. If that is absolutely impossible for you, then schedule yourself a lunch break. Just be prepared, as it could cost you a paid appointment.

Like talking on the phone, eating during a session looks horrible. You can't possibly be attentive while consuming a meal, no matter what the meal is. It's also distracting and unsanitary. A trainer I used to know frequently enjoyed bags of salad while working with her clients. This trainer didn't understand why it bothered the other trainers. "Salad is healthy, isn't it?" she'd say, wiping shining gobs of low-fat dressing from her chin, spraying tiny bits of onions as she spoke.

Another trainer I know ordered a bacon, egg, and cheese sandwich to a personal training session. He was a senior trainer at this particular club. I believe the client paid around $100 for the workout. When the food arrived, he stepped away from the client and walked across the gym to pay the delivery guy. When he returned, he said "Do ten more," and leaned against the wall, loudly chomping at his breakfast. After much struggling and some difficulty, the client finished his set and racked up the weight on his own. Everyone around but the trainer was uncomfortable.

These are both extreme cases, but munching on a protein bar isn't any better. Stay away from food. Breath mints are okay. If you need to consume something during a session, keep a drink handy, like water.

3. DON'T pretend to be something you're not.

Sometimes in our eagerness to please all the people all the time (it can't be done) we bite off more than we can chew. It's usually not the trainer's fault. Most health clubs and employers in the fitness world encourage it. Maybe a trainer took an online course that told him he is now certified in kickboxing, or Pilates, or whatever. Maybe she took an in-house kettlebell class from a joker who taught explicitly bad form. Whatever the reason, we should all be capable and confident before claiming to be anything.

If you're not a yoga expert, then don't pretend you are. There's nothing wrong with doing a "Yoga-inspired" session if you absolutely feel you must, but don't advertise yourself as the real deal if you're not. Be honest. As a former "certified" boxing instructor myself, I used to tell potential clients that I was absolutely not a fighter and I was not capable of teaching them the real sport of boxing or any true techniques of the "sweet science." However, I could give them a "boxing-inspired cardio workout." I met all client expectations (refer back to Chapter 7) and was completely honest. Most of the time, my clients loved it! But I'm still not a boxer.

WHEN I MEET A POTENTIAL CLIENT INTERESTED IN BOXING, I REFER THEM TO A QUALIFIED INSTRUCTOR.

An even better policy is to show the potential client your real strengths (and of course, how pleasant you can be for the duration of the session.) Chances are that they only want to try a particular mode of exercise because a magazine or someone on TV recommended it. Find out what their goals are, and why they wanted to try that mode in the first place. You can always say something like "For us to get the most out of our time together, let's focus on the things that I can best help you with. I have some awesome recommendations!" Steer the workout in a way to give them the best experience. Make them work. Build a relationship.

These days, I don't ever offer a "boxing-inspired cardio workout." I offer what I'm good at. Nine out of ten times, the client is sold on Danny the Trainer. One out of ten, if they still want to box, I refer them to a qualified instructor.

4. DON'T have a client do a move that you have never done.

Too many times, a trainer can be seen putting clients through exercises that the trainer himself has obviously never tried. It is impossible to know the subtleties of a movement without having experienced it. Don't be in a rush to show off that "new" move you saw on YouTube. First become good at it. Then become good at working on it with others, such as friends and fellow trainers. Then, if it is appropriate, try it with a client.

There is a lot more to some exercises than meets the eye. Make sure you have a solid understanding of the mechanics.

THE KETTLEBELL SWING IS AN OFTEN MISUNDERSTOOD EXERCISE. MANY TRAINERS TEACH IT POORLY BECAUSE THEY THEMSELVES NEVER LEARNED IT WELL.

5. DON'T mislead your clients about what they can accomplish.

We shouldn't tell our client who only trains once a week that they will soon be performing sets of twenty uninterrupted pull-ups or squatting 400 lbs. While I encourage trainers to think and talk big with their clients, we must always be realistic. I am all about making bold statements about the future as well as the present, but I never lie to anybody.

Many people will come to you for weight loss, but you can't train your way out of a poor diet. Let your client know that. Don't make fake promises and say they can achieve results without doing their part when you're not there. You want them to make progress. If they do, they will keep training and you will continue to get paid. Tell them in a roundabout way that you cannot help them lose weight--or anything for that matter--unless they are on board as much as you are. If presented properly, this accountability should empower them.

My brother and fellow trainer, Al Kavadlo, once even told a client "It's not my job to get you results." Damn. That's the complete *opposite* of what most trainers claim! But it's the truth, and as Al will be the first to tell you, the truth hurts. In this situation it was exactly what the client needed to hear. There are situations where being less blunt is appropriate.

Think about it; how can anyone realistically commit to getting someone else results in one or two hours a week. That leaves one-hundred and sixty-six hours unaccounted for, and you don't even know this person! Always be honest about what you can achieve.

AL KAVADLO ALWAYS TELLS THE TRUTH: "IT'S NOT MY JOB TO GET YOU RESULTS." IT'S YOUR JOB! THE TRAINER IS THERE TO HELP BUT NO ONE CAN DO THE WORK FOR YOU.

6. DON'T make up answers to things you don't know.

For some reason, whether it's about exercise, science, sports, or what-have-you, many trainers can't stop themselves from making up answers to questions when they do not know the real answer. Yes, it is tempting to always want to come off like an expert, especially when someone is paying for your expertise, but as any expert will admit, it's impossible to truly know everything. (One could argue that it's impossible to truly know *anything*, for that matter.)

Your client will respect you more if you tell them that you don't know the answer to a particular question, but that you will find out. Then actually try to find out.

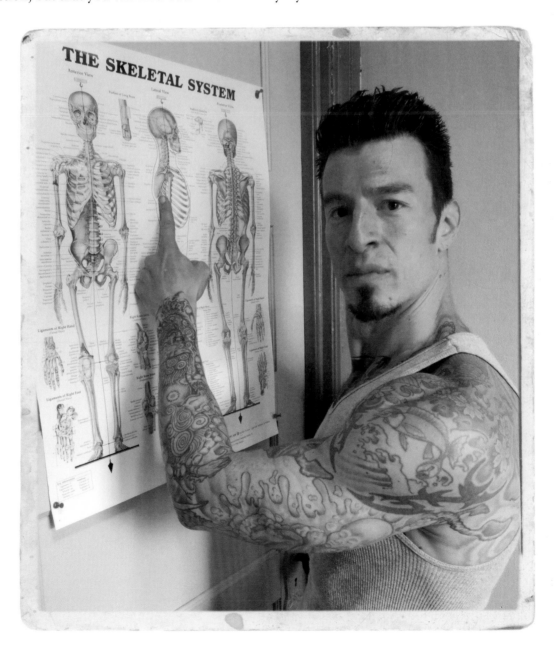

7. DON'T cancel/reschedule your appointments last-minute.

When you cancel or reschedule appointments, you not only send the message that cancelling is okay, you practically encourage it. You can never fault your client for cancelling on you last minute, if it is something that you do to them. There is not much to say here.

This behavior is inexcusable for professionals. Show up when you say you will show up and stay organized.

8. DON'T spend extra time on first workouts. Spend less.

When I managed trainers, one of my tasks was to walk the training floor and observe the goings on of the gym. I really liked this. My favorite part was observing the first workouts. I always knew when the prospective client was going to sign on for training. It was obvious every time. I didn't have to hear what was being said between the trainer and trainee to know. Ninety percent of communication is non-verbal; I simply read the body language.

There was a new trainer who seemed to be the total package: he was good looking, pleasant, and gave quality workouts. I'd glance over at the session half way through and I'd say to myself "Oh yeah, that person is buying." When I would look again ten minutes before the session's scheduled end, I'd be certain the prospect would sign on. The trainer and trainee were enjoying the workout, making eye contact, laughing together, and establishing a rapport. He would put the prospect on the stretch table and stretch the hamstrings.

Then the quads.

The glutes.

It would be time for the first workout to end. Then he'd stretch the biceps.

The triceps.

Shoulders.

Neck.

Seventy minutes into the encounter I could see the prospect's face go from "This is awesome. I need training bad!" to "Uh, okay... I gotta go..."

No joke, sometimes these workouts went on for an hour and a half. I know if I'm in a gym for an hour and a half, I can't wait to get the hell outta there, and I'm someone who loves to work out! Imagine how the prospect feels; they probably don't even like the gym, but signed on anyway. They wisely accepted the offer for a training session, and although it goes great, it never seems to end. After ninety minutes (or any more than an hour,) there is no way they want to talk about coming back or buying. They don't want to book a follow-up. They're late to meet their friend for happy hour and they're ready to leave. Wrap it up.

I actually believe that if anything, first workouts should be truncated. Mine rarely last more than forty-five minutes. A new client and I do everything that is appropriate and nothing more. I assess and challenge them, always having them work harder than they are used to. I show my new clients what it's like to train with me but I leave them wanting more. Their legs may be sore as hell after a first workout but they still can't wait to come back. Rather than wishing the session would end, they can't believe how quickly it went.

9. DON'T devalue your training.

The first person who ever tattooed me back in 1991, the now-famous Coney Island Vinnie, had a sign hanging on the wall of his shop that contained a quote from legendary tattoo artist "Sailor Jerry" Collins. It read:

"Good work ain't cheap and cheap work ain't good. You get what you pay for."

THIS IS JUST AS TRUE FOR PERSONAL TRAINING AS IT IS FOR TATTOOING.

Enforce your rate. Yes, I know you are probably used to getting pimped out by the gym, but trust me on this one. Your clients will pay what is fair and respect you for it. There are rookie trainers who charge $40 a session and expert trainers who charge hundreds. But I assure you there are no experienced, quality personal trainers charging $40 and everybody knows it. Charge what is appropriate and stick with it. Naturally, the appropriate rate may vary based on your geography, the time of day, the caliber of your training, and of course supply and demand. Find your price and stand your ground. Every now and again you will need to negotiate. That's okay; it's something every career personal trainer in the world has done at times. Negotiating can be crucial for picking up new business. But remember: You are not prepared to negotiate if you are not prepared to walk away. By the same token…

10. DON'T kid yourself either.

The restaurants that sell a porterhouse steak for $100 have a better product than the ones that sell a prime rib for $6.99. When I started out in a chain gym, I was the guy who agreed to train every new member who had a workout coming to them. I did not make any money from these first workouts, just the chance to acquire a new client. 6am on a Monday? I'm your guy. 9pm on a Friday? You got it. 7am the next day? Yes indeed. I was the cheap Vegas prime rib and I would have had no business presenting myself as Brooklyn's Peter Luger Steak House.

Of course I tried to sign everyone up, and I was extremely successful much of the time by using the first workout methods described in this book (See Appendix A.) But when I was starting out, the

clients I signed up payed "entry level" trainer rates, and therefore my payout was low. Yet at the time it would have been absurd for me to demand more. How could I? Trainers that command a higher rate don't do complementary workouts during peak hours because they have paying clients at those times. They command a higher rate. This is economics-- supply and demand. Your fee cannot be an arbitrary or ideal number; people have to be willing to pay it, and you must be able to look them in the eye and confidently pitch it.

CHAPTER 11

SNAPPY ANSWERS TO LOADED QUESTIONS

> "SOMETIMES THE QUESTIONS
> ARE COMPLICATED BUT
> THE ANSWERS ARE SIMPLE."
> -DR. SEUSS

There is no doubt that at some point in your career you will hear some or all of the following questions. Logic is not always the best way to respond. It's important to know how to handle these difficult, yet often asked inquiries so that they don't catch you off guard. In compiling this section, I consulted with some of New York City's top personal trainers, and though we've had varying degrees of success with these and similar responses, the answers presented here are all better than saying something you will regret. But like personal training, they are not guaranteed. Let's take a look.

Q: "I put on muscle so fast. If I lift any weight I'll blow up. What can I do that won't make me huge?"

A: "Good question. While it is true that different bodies put on muscle faster than others and we all have different body compositions, we will not let that stand in our way. Continue to be open with me and we will handle your individual needs accordingly. If you feel like you're gaining too much muscle, let me know and we'll make adjustments. (This probably won't happen.) Let's try it. I've been doing this a long time and I know how to help you."

Trainer Talk:

This is a tough question to field. It's generally hard for trainers to deal with clients who say that they put on muscle (bulk up) too quickly. Those of us who work out know how hard the big guys train and eat to put on size, and how silly it sounds when folks say they're scared of developing a big, strong, muscular physique by accident. But the clients who are new to exercise don't know that. Let's be sensitive to their feelings, as it's not their fault they've been misled.

We need to be honest but not to offend. With this response, I managed to be kind, while saying nothing but the truth. Still, I was supportive and motivational and used the words "our" and "we" a lot. It's best to stay positive and suggest modifications to diet (like eating more fruits and veggies) without coming on too strong or judgmental, particularly in the beginning. Avoid heavy weight training with this client in favor of bodyweight exercise.

EVERYBODY NEEDS A FRUIT BOWL.

Q: "Aren't squats bad for your knees?"

A: "I understand your concern. Squats are potentially dangerous because many people do them poorly. But we will make sure we do them right. Anything is bad... potentially. People die in plane crashes. Are planes always bad? You can choke on spinach. Is it bad for you? What if you get injured saving someone's life. Is saving lives bad? I once read in the paper that a man suffered a heart attack while making love... Well, you get the point."

Trainer Talk:

As a trainer part of your job is to make sure that your clients are performing exercises safely. Barbell squats require attentive spotting even for experienced lifters, which, whoever asked this question, clearly is not. It goes without saying that safety comes first. You are a professional personal trainer.

Squatting is one of our largest and oldest movement patterns, not to mention one of the classic exercises. Humans learn to squat before they can run, or even walk. It's in our DNA; all primates do it. If a client tells me that squats feel "unnatural," it's usually because he or she trained themselves not to squat by sitting on their ass for years, hunched over. Squats strengthen almost every muscle in the body and encourage both neurological and cardiovascular health. Squats have helped many people with bad knees get strong again. In fact, barring injuries or other such physical limitations, I believe that NOT DOING SQUATS is bad for your knees!

SQUATS ARE GOOD FOR YOUR KNEES.

"Look at all this belly fat!?! Shouldn't we do more crunches?!?"

"That's a really great question! I understand why you would think that. Our generation was brought up to believe that crunches will reduce fat along the midsection but it's not true. It turns out that muscle and fat are two completely different compositions. Fat can never turn into muscle and muscle can never turn into fat, no matter how many crunches we do. Sure doing ab-work will sculpt and firm the muscle beneath the fat, but reduction comes down to diet and overall energy expenditure. It's impossible to spot-reduce body fat."

 While crunches do have their place, if we really want exercise to contribute to decreased body fat, then we have two main approaches:

1. Do More Big Movements

Full-body exercises expend more energy than smaller, isolated ones, and moving burns more calories than resting. It's extremely subjective what the best exercises are, but five good deadlifts can do more for your abs than a hundred crunches. Recruiting so many muscles at the same time burns more energy, instead of storing it. The full body tension also gives your abs a hell of a workout.

Never start an abs program without giving attention to low back and glutes as well. Incorporating deadlifts (and/or bridgework, floor levers, planks, hyper-extension, and more) will ensure that you do not ignore these areas. Neglecting the posterior chain is like training the right side of your body but not the left.

2. Increase Lean Muscle

Being more muscular helps speed the metabolism (We may want to mention this to the client who asked the first question as well.) I'm sure you've heard that a body with a high ratio of lean muscle mass has a faster metabolism than a fatty, less muscular body. This is usually true. Help your client build some muscle and they will get leaner as long as they don't start eating more.

Only when the body fat is below a certain unhealthy point will anyone get to see the results of exercises that sculpt and tone the abs. If that's the goal then do it right. Work leg raises and transverse exercises along with those beloved crunches. Again, crunches are fine for someone who cannot do hanging windshield wiper abs, but the larger movements are more favorable. Generally when floor abs get too easy, try them on a decline bench. After that, move on to hanging abs. My thoughts on abs and specific routines could fill a book much larger than this one so I'll stop right here and move on.

Get comfortable saying the phrase "it's impossible" (as in "It's impossible to spot reduce body fat.") Practice saying it in front of a mirror. You want to sound like an authority when you use those words. They can sometimes be the best comeback.

NEITHER THE MIGHTY
WINDSHIELD WIPER...

...NOR THE BASIC SIT-UP CAN
SPOT-REDUCE BODY FAT

Q: "I need to lose weight so I signed up for a half Marathon. Cardio is the best thing for weight loss, right?"

A: "There is no 'best thing' for weight loss, but if pressed to give an answer, I'd have to go with eating less."

Trainer Talk: I believe that the single most important decision we can make regarding our health is the food we put in our bodies. If we want to lose weight, then we need to eat accordingly. Your client can start eating better by avoiding packaged and processed foods that use low quality ingredients manufactured in a lab. Cooking and buying their own ingredients is the best way for your clients to know what they're actually putting in their bodies. A good rule of thumb is to eat foods made by a person not a company, in a kitchen not a factory.

Suggest that your client eat an apple and something green every single day and avoid processed wheat and sugar products. Portion sizes are out of control, so clients should be mindful of how much goes on their plate in the first place. That will help them lose excess body weight more effectively than any exercise program, even running or jumping rope (both of which are phenomenal.) Exercise has unlimited other benefits like increased strength, endurance, attractiveness, wellness, and empowerment, but if the goal is simply pound reduction, clients must also eat less.

WHEN IT COMES TO WEIGHT LOSS, EATING LESS IS EVEN BETTER THAN CARDIO.

Q: "How long before I can do a pistol squat?" (Or press 300 lbs, or fit into that dress again, or execute ten pull-ups, etc.)

A: "That's up to you and how dedicated you are."

Trainer Talk: As much as I enjoy living in the present, I must accept that I live in a very goal-centric culture. We are constantly being exposed to bogus claims of instant physical transformations. It is important to remind ourselves and our clients that these claims are complete and unadulterated bullshit. It is pure marketing designed solely with the goal of selling a product, not telling the truth. That is where we come in. I make it a point to tell new clients that it takes at least three months for the body to manifest any real change. Think about it; how fast can living matter actually transform? How rapidly can new skills realistically be acquired? How quickly can proprioception evolve? Change does not happen overnight. It's important to be process oriented not just goal oriented.

People are often shocked when I tell them that certain goals can take months or even years to attain. Sometimes they don't believe me, but it doesn't matter. That's the beauty of it. You can't fake the funk. If your client wants to do their first muscle-up, go down a pants size, or increase their one rep max, they must put forth the effort. There is no other way. No shortcuts.

THE PISTOL SQUAT IS AN EXERCISE THAT DEMANDS BEING FOCUSED ON THE PROCESS RATHER THAN THE GOAL.

Q: "Am I eating enough carbs?"

A: "Yes."

Trainer Talk: Because we are taught that complex carbohydrates are our most efficient source of energy, many people think that if we stop flooding our systems with them non-stop, we will pass out from exhaustion due to performing everyday activities. We won't.

Processed carbs (even ones that boast "whole grain") deliver very little nutrition. It's been ground out of them. That's why they're often fortified with water-soluble vitamins that get pissed out. These products contribute to peaks and dips in energy, bloated bellies, and swollen joints. Instruct your client to pay attention to how many of these items they're consuming. A bagel for breakfast, a sandwich for lunch, and pasta for dinner really add up.

Fruits, vegetables, and legumes are carbohydrates that do not fall into this category. Bread, rice, and pasta do. I don't mean to imply that your client can never have a piece of bread again. In fact some real bread (the kind with 5 or 6 ingredients, not 20) or steal-cut oats are fine from time to time. But lots of people need to cut down and they don't even know it.

The same thing applies to so-called "sports drinks." They are no better than sodas. These beverages were designed for sports teams that practice for hours on end in intense weather. Most human beings don't fall into this category. For almost all your clients, water is best.

THESE LOW QUALITY GRAIN PRODUCTS ARE FOR THE BIRDS.

APPLES GIVE
YOU ABS.

"Can you just show me how to work the machines?"

 "No."

Trainer Talk: Personal training does not mean walking someone around the gym to point to and talk about large, heavy pieces of equipment. If this is what a potential client wants, then explain to them that this is not what we do. Then show them what we do. Give them a workout they cannot do without you and start building that relationship.

A technique I have used in the past when faced with this question is sheer, unbridled honesty. (It's the best policy.) I explain to potential clients that most of these machines are probably not optimal for them in the first place. Usually when you tell someone that compound movements and dietary adjustments will help them get leaner than lying hamstring curls will, they want to hear more.

TRY SAYING SOMETHING LIKE THIS:

"SINCE WE HAVE THE OPPORTUNITY TO WORK TOGETHER TODAY, HOW ABOUT I SHOW YOU WHAT CAN HELP YOU [INSERT GOAL HERE] IN THE BEST WAY POSSIBLE? LET'S MAKE THE MOST OF OUR TIME TOGETHER!"

There is lots of information available on the internet, in bookstores, and in manuals about machines. The potential client has always had access to it and has never chosen to act. You saying it one more time will make no difference. Show them the ways that we can make a difference. Get them up (and out of the machine) and give them the Trainer Experience!

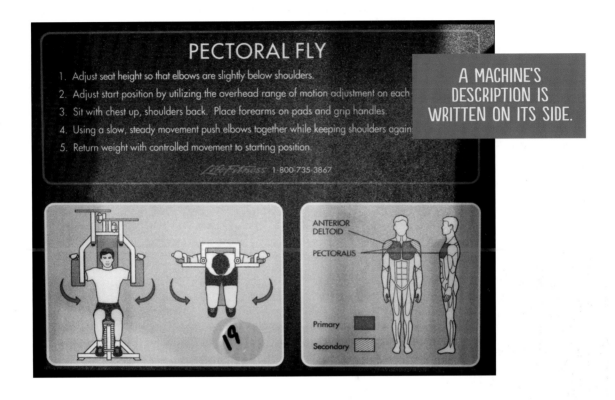

CHAPTER 12

MORE ON PERSONAL TRAINING SALES

"YOU WILL GET ALL YOU WANT IN LIFE, IF YOU HELP
ENOUGH OTHER PEOPLE GET WHAT THEY WANT."
-ZIG ZIGLAR

The truth is that when we sell personal training, we are helping someone get what they want. They come to us, understandably confused, often out of desperation. Somehow our paths crossed and here we are together. Don't let the prospective client (PC) take the easy way out, continuing to grow weaker as they grow older. Help them take a stand; they need you! They wouldn't be standing there if they believed you couldn't help them, would they?

These gentle creatures have a spectacular opportunity in front of them: hiring you! One could easily make the argument that the ability to keep PC's from walking out the door is the most important skill a personal trainer can have.

The subject of selling personal training can and has filled many books. For these pages, I decided to stay away from rote dialog and premeditated scripts whenever possible, preferring to go with general principles and applications. This is because the actual words you say barely even matter. In reality, we have been talking about sales all along. Every single interaction that you and your client have together is part of the sales process.

If I can put forth one main point in this chapter, it is that selling is all about building a bond—getting the customer to be comfortable. One of the best ways to immediately go about this is to talk about what they want to talk about, even if it has nothing to do with fitness. Show enthusiasm for what they say. Establishing things in common is the cornerstone of a relationship. Hear them out respectfully and pay attention. Maintain eye contact and smile. Know their name. Mirror their body language. These are the reasons that two trainers can say the same words and give the same workouts, but one will close the sale time after time, while the other will not.

I intend to give you some broad strokes that can be adapted to many situations, but there are no guarantees. Selling is an art form that takes time and experience to hone. Yes, some people are born with more sales charisma than others but you don't become an expert salesman until you've pitched hundreds of people in hundreds of situations. Like everything in life, you get better at selling the more you do it.

First Things First

If you work for a gym, the PC probably has to fill out a PAR-Q or other such pre-workout health screening. This is a simple set of questions that many certifying bodies agree are important to ask before starting a fitness program. All of my private personal training clients fill out a PAR-Q before embarking on a program with me, and I do not currently work for a gym. This is a good practice, but it's best kept short. Unless you are given a reason to probe deeper, ask only the minimum required. I recently observed a trainer grilling a client about possible injuries during what appeared to be their first encounter. After the client told him he was injury-free, the trainer continued to ask "What about your lower back?"

"No issues."

"Knees?"

"Fine too."

"Shoulders ok?"

"Yup."

WHICH SCENARIO MORE LIKELY TO LEAD TO A SALE? THIS...

Mind you, this exchange took place after the PC already filled out a long questionnaire. The interrogation went on for an uncomfortably long amount of time. It was as if the trainer was trying to talk him out of training by making the experience so unpleasant. I could see the sale slip away like dust in the wind.

...OR THIS?

The point of asking questions is not to show how many body parts one can name. It is to:

1. Make sure it is physically safe for your client to train.

2. Find the most appropriate way of training your client.

3. Establish trust and comfort from the beginning.

That's it. In the rare case that there is an injury or issue, I usually quote the immortal Jack LaLane and tell my future client: "You have 640 muscles in your body. There may be a few exercises you can't do but there are hundreds you can." Then we move right on to a stellar workout.

The Workout

It should be a given that the workout itself will be solid. All client expectations and professionalisms dealt with in this volume (punctuality, attentiveness, physical and verbal cuing, etc.) should be met and exceeded. This chapter is about the sale. Refer back to Chapters 8-10 for more about the training session.

Check out Appendix B for some sample routines, but please don't feel the need to execute them exactly as written. Train for the client in front of you. It's impossible to have a completely predetermined workout that works the same for everybody.

One more thing: Avoid using equipment that requires a pin. You want the trainee to be sold on you, not a machine. If I give a workout, I don't want my PC to think:

"Woah! My legs are cooked! Those leg extensions kicked my ass! Can't wait to train again!"

I'd rather hear:

"Woah! My legs are cooked! Danny Kavadlo kicked my ass! Can't wait to train again!"

See the difference?

The less equipment you use, the better. Yes there are a few cases where isolation machines can be the most suitable exercise for elderly or injured clients. (Body builders too, but they make unlikely first workouts.) But most of the time, keep the use of equipment to a minimum.

MOST OF THE TIME,
KEEP THE USE OF
EQUIPMENT TO A
MINIMUM.

Early and Often

I encourage trainers to ask for the sale early and often. Sales are frequently lost simply because they aren't brought up enough, if ever. A friend and colleague of mine recommends hearing the word "no" seven times before moving along. While I try not to get into exact numbers (sometimes it's one; sometimes it is indeed seven or more) I must admit that the "Seven Time Rule" is good advice for trainers, particularly when starting out. It's hard to stay focused when you hear "no" a lot, as all new trainers do. There was a time when every successful trainer, including myself, heard ten "no's for every "yes." Stay positive. I know it's difficult, but get in the habit of asking for the sale frequently.

Even if the PC says no, since you asked for the sale early, you have plenty more chances to try again. Has a server at a restaurant ever asked if you wanted a drink? If you said no, he or she probably returned shortly to ask if you were sure. Then asked once more when the food arrived. By this point, it's likely you broke down and said yes. Ask for the sale often.

ALL TRAINERS HAVE HEARD THE WORD "NO" A LOT. DON'T TAKE IT PERSONALLY.

Sale Ends Soon

The chances of acquiring a new client drop substantially the second they walk out the door. This is why gyms offer "limited time" discounts. Have you ever noticed how every month is a sale? It adds a sense of urgency. There are gyms everywhere and a new one seems to pop up every day. If a PC is wondering about other gyms in the area before signing on, what's to stop them from leaving? Why should they go with you anyway? Urgency. Many gyms use the "Sale Ends Soon" tactic to lock down a potential member right now. The gyms know what they're doing. When a customer is under the impression that today is the "Last Day" to get the best rate, they are more likely to sign on right now. This technique will help you get clients too. No matter what someone says, once they leave, it is hard to get them back. You never know what's going to happen. They can come home to an IRS bill, a dent in the car, or a flood in the basement. Giving a deadline helps seal the deal of a lifetime.

After you agree on which training package, and you shake hands or high-5 your new client, tell them to go get their credit card or checkbook right now. Don't be too aggressive, but you may have to be a little aggressive. Such is life. If they say their credit card is in their locker, and they'll do it after they take a shower, tell them you won't still be there. They must go get it now. You will wait for them. Everything can change in five minutes so it's best to capitalize on how good they feel from working out. If they say they will pay on the way out, tell them it will only take a moment and it is important to do it right now. Do not give this responsibility of completing the transaction to the front desk staff, as they will probably mess it up. In life and sales, if you do not personally make sure something happens, it most likely will not.

Volume Discount

When a client buys a group of training sessions at a reduced per-session rate (Never say "price;" instead say rate, amount, or investment) it is called a volume discount. For example, one session costs $115. That's an awesome rate, but if you sign up for twenty-five, that same session costs only $99 (you save $400.) Fifty is just $88 each (you save $1,350.) Ask the PC is they'd like to save $400 or $1,350 and see what they say. Almost all gyms offer a volume discount. Once again, it is all about ensuring the sale.

Volume discounts work great in the club for two main reasons.

1. They bring in a lot of money.

Look at the previous example. Instead of asking if PC wanted to spend $2,475 or $4,400, we asked if they want to save $400 or $1,350. Hell, they can save close to three grand if they buy 100 up front (just $82 per session) right now. Phrasing the same question differently makes the larger package more enticing. It brings in more immediate cash, which is the gym's goal. It is a store.

2. Large packages can help the trainer too.

Selling multiple sessions in a single transaction is about as close to a guarantee as we can get in terms of retaining a client for a predetermined duration. If they paid for six months or a year up front, they tend to see it through most of the time. But you never know. I once sold 100 hours of personal training to a great lead for $10,900 and she only trained once. It was great for the gym, as they kept all the money (rightly so,) but not so great for the trainer, who got paid around $50 for the single hour she trained.

Basically, a volume discount is good in the gym because it helps trainers get business and clubs hit goals, but it has a potential downside. Sometimes a gym will sell a large volume of sessions at a rate that is below the trainer's standard wage. Don't get me wrong; this makes sense in many situations, particularly if the trainer is new and needs business. But I've seen it also happen to high-producing trainers. When their veteran services are sold at rookie rates without their consent, it helps only the establishment, not the trainer. It needs to do both.

Volume discounts can be more favorable to trainers who work for a gym than to the self-employed, but there are pros and cons to each. The following two situations require different approaches to volume discounts.

1. Cancellation Policy

In most cases, when a client cancels a personal training session without ample notice, they are charged for the session. Of course there are exceptions to every rule such as illness and emergencies. Barring those situations, however, if you turned down Client A at 7am because you were booked with Client B, and Client B no-shows, we all agree that you should be paid. Even Client B would agree at the time (although he may not later.)

It is company policy at most clubs to deduct directly from the training package at the time of the cancellation. I charged my clients (maybe too often, with too few exceptions) for late cancellations when I worked at the gym, but now, as an independent trainer, it's not so black and white. While it used to be easy to pawn this practice off as company policy, the relationship changes when the company is you. Without the buffer of "management," the strictness of the rule feels more subjective to independent trainers, who sometimes let their clients get away with too much. But you must stay true to your policy. Your time is valuable. Do not allow your clients to take advantage of you.

My current approach rests somewhere in the middle. I sometimes let it slide the first time someone late-cancels on me. I call it a "First Time Violation." It shows the client that I'm a good guy who's on their side, while also expressing that they will definitely be charged should it happen again.

2. Expiration Date

Like the cancellation policy, this helps in the gym, but it's tricky on your own. When a gym sells a block of sessions, the client has a certain amount of time to use them or they expire. I do not like enforcing that as an independent trainer. Whereas it's perfectly logical in the gym, it's hard to look a client in the eye and say "I haven't seen you in three months. I'm keeping your $1,000." But it must happen sometimes. That's one of the reasons I do not recommend selling large packages up front if you work for yourself.

Also, trainers who work for someone else usually get paid per hour that they train no matter how many hours the client has purchased. For the independent trainer, however, you get the payment for a big package up front, which can mean months before you get paid again. That's the other reason I don't recommend it.

These days my rate is my rate. I tell my new clients that they can pay for several sessions up front but the per-session rate will not change. It is sometimes more convenient for them to buy in bulk so I grant it, but I prefer when they pay one to two sessions at a time (even though when I worked at gyms I liked to sell the largest packages possible.)

Tier Drop

This may be hard to grasp if you have never worked for a gym. We have referenced trainer levels previously. The term "tier" means the same as "level." In a nutshell, the trainers that command a higher rate are top tier (or high level.) The trainers that do not (often, but not always new trainers) are low level. There are usually between 3-5 different levels and price points. It is very common for even a top tier trainer to have a few clients that pay a "discount" (lower tier) rate. The trainer makes less money off these clients, usually getting paid like a junior trainer for these sessions. Sometimes it is worthwhile to take on lower-paying clients, like if they want to train off-

-peak hours and the trainer has a gap in his or her schedule. Other times it's not. The terms "tier" and "level" refer to terms used in health clubs specifically, but dropping your price per session as an independent trainer is the same thing as taking on a lower level client in the club.

To make larger packages more enticing, trainers are sometimes advised to drop a level in addition to the volume discount. For example, one level IV session costs $115. Ten level IV sessions cost $1,050 (save $100.) But ten Level III sessions cost $950. If you cannot close the sale for $1,050, consider dropping a level. Ask the future client, "If I can knock $100 off right now, would you do it?" If they say yes (and you don't have someone better in their desired timeslot,) then it's probably worth it even if you make $10 less per session. It's better than zero. When I would offer this discount, I'd refer to it as a "first-time buyer's" discount, so the client would not expect to get the same rate upon renewal. (There is no reason to get into levels in this situation as it often confuses the client.) I would explain that this is the only time they will ever get this price, so they should go big. Different clubs have different policies, so it is a good idea to consult with your PT Manager about the game plan.

Never tell a client that their savings usually affect your payout; it's tacky. But let them know their discounted rate will go up.

Never Judge A Book by Its Cover

Pitch your services to everybody in the gym, even if it looks like they don't want training or can't afford it. Years ago I worked with a gentleman who industry insiders (myself included) consider the best General Manager in New York. Together we once sold 4 years of membership, 200 hours of highest level personal training, and a massage package to a gentleman who some may have thought looked homeless. When it came time to process the transaction (Never say "contract;" instead say paperwork, agreement, or registration form) our scraggly newfound friend reached into his plastic bag (no wallet) and pulled out his black Amex, a card which one must spend $250,000 annually to even qualify for. Needless to say, it was approved for over $24,000. I was glad we asked for the sale. And he was happy to sign on for world-class training at one of New York's best facilities.

This was an extreme case but you'd be surprised. Assume everyone has a black Amex.

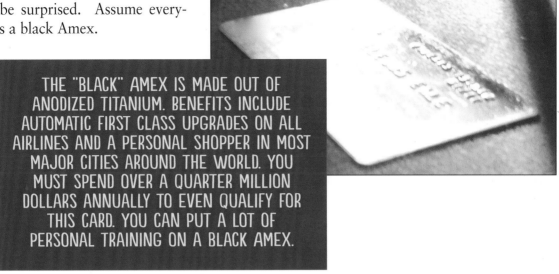

THE "BLACK" AMEX IS MADE OUT OF ANODIZED TITANIUM. BENEFITS INCLUDE AUTOMATIC FIRST CLASS UPGRADES ON ALL AIRLINES AND A PERSONAL SHOPPER IN MOST MAJOR CITIES AROUND THE WORLD. YOU MUST SPEND OVER A QUARTER MILLION DOLLARS ANNUALLY TO EVEN QUALIFY FOR THIS CARD. YOU CAN PUT A LOT OF PERSONAL TRAINING ON A BLACK AMEX.

Closing Time

From the initial handshake to the swipe of the credit card, everything you say and do will affect the outcome of a sale. Throughout the experience, we made it a point to ask the right questions (see Chapter 4.) Up until now, that meant open ended questions that get the client talking, as opposed to questions with short "yes" or "no" answers. In contrast, however, when it's time for the final act, we actually *want* a short answer, specifically "yes."

"Do you think this type of workout will help you?"

"Do you think you will get results if we did this three times a week?"

"Did it feel good to do more chin-ups than you ever thought you could?"

These are all affirmative questions. All the answers are obviously yes. Good. We want our future client to be comfortable saying yes when it's time to ask for the credit card.

At the gym, there will be many combinations of packages and levels. Even if you work for yourself, it's likely that you offer discounts and incentives. With many options, it's best to offer few: no more than two or three choices. Giving too many choices often makes it harder to decide. Think of a menu at a restaurant. It takes much longer to pick one item out of thirty than it does to pick one out of ten.

You should already know which training package to pitch because we have been asking the right questions and listening carefully to the answers all along. For example, if you and your future client have been talking about training three times a week, it would be silly to offer a five-session package. They would burn through it too quickly and you'd have to sell them all over again. Similarly, if your client wants to work out with you only once in a while, don't offer a hundred-pack. That would make no sense and scare them away.

Generally, when offered three choices, most folks will pick the one in the middle (Offer ten, twenty-five, or fifty sessions in the first example.) If you offer two, make sure to pitch the one you think they will buy and one bigger. (Offer five or ten for the second.) The actual price is the last thing you discuss. After the pitch, stop talking. Whoever speaks first loses.

That's right. Ask for the sale and shut the fuck up. Maintain eye contact. Don't flinch. I have seen trainers literally talk potential clients out of a sale when they spoke too soon. It's true. Instead of shutting up, the trainer will say "Is it the money?" The client may have never even considered money, but hmmm, now that you mention it...

Don't suggest objections. Stand your ground and be confident. Desperation is a turn off. This is true in every situation in life.

The second the client consents to future training, congratulate them immediately. "Welcome to the world of personal training!" Shake their hand to seal the deal. High-5's and hugs all around! They can't back out now.

Fill out the PT agreement for them. Ask: "Last name? Spell it?" Move quickly. "Address?" Write it out and get the method of payment. When people see paperwork, they sometimes panic. Spare them the indignity. Finalize the sale and book the next session.

More Than Words

There are certain key phrases that you or your future client can say that almost guarantee the sale. The General Manager mentioned above had a knack for putting true words in such a way, as to get the client to simply say that buying makes sense. Genius.

For example, he'd say "You'll get the most out of your personal training if you do a massage package too. Every professional athlete in the world gets massage. I can save you the most money if we sign up for both right now."

The next words out of the client's mouth were usually "Okay. That makes sense." The few times that this wasn't the case, he'd follow up with something like: "Well why not? It's a no-brainer." Both "makes sense" and "no-brainer" yield the same result: they acknowledge that buying is a smart decision. It's understood that the client would be foolish not to do it, and no one wants to be a fool.

There are other times when a prospective client will ask "What do most people go with?" We love this question! It's a fact that most folks want to belong, so go with it. Make them feel like they're part of an elite club. People enjoy letting the decisions of other people affect their own. Hell, even if they don't ask this question, tell them anyway. Say "*All* of our savviest members do the _____ package we were just talking about!" Who doesn't want to be savvy?

Like the workout itself and the sales process up until now, we should never forget about non-verbal communication. Subtle things like mimicking your prospective client's tone and body language can help put them more at ease. If they're sitting up straight, then you sit up straight. If they are calm, then you be calm. If they are animated and using hand gestures, then you do the same. It's important to always be yourself, but adapt as necessary. Be your loud self when they're loud, your quiet self when they're quiet. Plus, remember to smile, be physically and mentally present, and make eye contact. (I never get tired of mentioning that.)

Personal training is an emotional buy. I mean, if people really thought about it rationally, they probably wouldn't do it. We have to appeal to their soul. We must shake them out of their coma and show them how good it feels to be alive! If I said "I'll stand here for $100 while you work out," I wouldn't have any takers. But when I wake up the sleeping giant that's been trapped in the man, then, and only then, do I have a shot. Fire up the emotions; pull at the heartstrings. Release the endorphins. Push the body and the spirit!

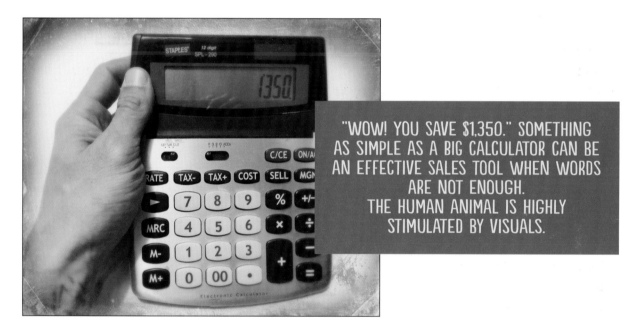

"WOW! YOU SAVE $1,350." SOMETHING AS SIMPLE AS A BIG CALCULATOR CAN BE AN EFFECTIVE SALES TOOL WHEN WORDS ARE NOT ENOUGH. THE HUMAN ANIMAL IS HIGHLY STIMULATED BY VISUALS.

Re-Butt

The subject of overcoming objections must be addressed. Here are the ones you will hear most often. I included a short, go-to response for each, as well a longer, more elaborate answer. While it's important to refute your future clients' fears, remember also to be sympathetic to their plight. Relate to them.

I recommend discussing these rebuttals with other trainers. Bounce ideas around and share your feedback with each other. Practice different scenarios and situations; get comfortable talking about these subjects. Don't use my scripts word for word or it will sound fake. Make the words yours.

1. "I don't have the time."

Short Answer: "We all have the time. We must find it."

Long Story: Like handling any objection, this can be a bit delicate. You see, people love to make themselves sound busier than they really are. However, it is generally not wise to call someone out so blatantly on their excuse-making. I know it's tempting to tell the PC that you wake up at 4:30am, work 12-hours, have a kid, go to school, and still find the time. You may want to bring up your clients who train at the crack of dawn because they work six days a week, ten hours a day, and still find the time. But don't. You catch more flies with honey than you do with vinegar.

Instead, try saying something more like this: "You are right. You don't have any time to waste. That's precisely why you need a trainer with experience—to get the most out of your workout time. We'll start with a small training package and see how that works. We can always do a larger package next time."

Book the next session.

2. "I can't afford to."

Short Answer: "You can't afford not to."

Long Story: This is the question many trainers are most afraid of. They shouldn't be. An objection to price can be considered the best one of all because we have plenty of wiggle room. There are numerous price points, packages, volume discounts, and tier drops. Ask the PC if the issue is with the overall amount of the package (if so, sell a smaller package) or the per-session rate (if so, sell a lower level.)

Like we talked about earlier, knocking a little bit off the top can mean the difference between getting a brand new client and having a gaping hole in your schedule. Yes, it's a sticky situation when you want to drop a level. After all, you've been saying that ten personal training sessions costs $1,050. Now you're saying it can cost less. It must be phrased in such a way as not to appear that you've been holding out all along.

"If I would save you $100 right now, could you do it?"
(wait for response)

"Let me check and see if it's even possible."

Walk away. If you can't find your boss, ask someone else (assistant manager, senior trainer, anyone.) The entire staff should know to say "Yes you have my approval" in a situation like this. Next, you turn away from your boss (or whoever), and toward your new client with a big thumbs-up and a giant smile. After a massive high-5, say "I got some great news! We can do it! Let's book the next session." It's a strange method, but certain situations call for it. The client was trying to talk himself out of making a great choice. He was scared to change for the better and was blaming cost. He needed your help in sticking with one of the best decisions he's ever made in his life. The next words out of his mouth will probably be thank you.

3. "I have to think about it."

Short Answer: "What's there to think about?"

Long Story: This is a situation where the client has no realistic objections, and must retreat home to think up a reason not to train. Luckily, we've been putting the teachings of this book into practice by asking the right questions all along. Now it may be time to repeat their own words back to them.

- "You told me you needed to do this."

- "You told me you wanted to be healthy for your new baby."

- "You told me you were committed this time."

- "You told me you are in the early stages of type II diabetes. It will get worse if we do not make changes now."

- "You just told me your girlfriend broke up with you and she already has a new man! What are you waiting for?!?"

Remember the Sale Ends Soon section of this chapter? Bring the urgency.

4. "I'm gonna try it on my own."

Short Answer: "How's that been workin' for ya?"

Long Story: Obviously, trying it on their own has not been working. If it was, the PC would not be standing in front of you. However to avoid being insulting, let's tone it down a bit. I like to draw an analogy between lessons of any sort and personal training. Although I do not consider personal training sessions to be lessons per se, it is still a valid comparison that many can relate to.

The first time I went skiing, it was the best snow Vermont had seen in years so my friends and I decided to make a road trip. The resort was gorgeous and covered in fresh powder. It had all the makings of an epic weekend, except for the fact that I did nothing but bust my ass and get frustrated for the next forty-eight hours. Like a damn fool, I turned down the introductory lesson package.

I relate this story to my future client. I explain that when I went back the following year, I took the lessons and had an incredible time. More so, I gained skills that will remain with me. I ask the client which type of ski trip they want the gym to be epic or frustrating? I explain once again how I can help them. Then I repeat their words back to them as if they'd said "I have to think about it."

You do not have to use the ski story. Ask if they've ever taken lessons on a musical instrument or studied a foreign language. Those are great comparisons too.

The Tao Of The T.O.

If for whatever reason, you cannot finalize the sale on your own, then it's a good idea to bring in a veteran manager, trainer, or sales rep to take over or "T.O." Most experienced players enjoy selling and will be glad to assist. One thing though: if you bring anyone in for a T.O. you can't be mad at what they sell for you. You waive that right.

For example, a trainer wants to a sell twenty-five session package but is incapable of making it happen. After fifteen minutes, he feels the deal slipping away, so he brings in his manager who (after having to establish a bond of his own with the PC) is able to close the deal right then and there for ten sessions. "Congratulations!" Handshakes and high-5's all around! But later on, instead of being grateful, the trainer says "Hey, what did you do?!? I was gonna sell him twenty-five!?!" Bullshit. If the trainer could have sold twenty-five, he would have. If someone helps you sell, then watch and learn. Be happy the sale was not lost altogether.

Finally, I'd like to say that if you absolutely cannot close the sale today, but you believe that ultimately you can, then book a follow-up appointment. Refer to it as a "tentative" follow-up if your PC is reluctant. Whether they schedule it or not, call the next day to see how they're doing. Give them a chance to speak. Be positive. Again, ask a nice, open ended question:

"Hey Joe, it's Danny from the gym. You killed it yesterday! I just wanted to check in and see how you're feeling after the workout."

It is good to remain on good terms and let PC's know you're there for them in the future, even if they can't hire you right now. You never know. Birthdays, anniversaries, and holidays will come eventually. Maybe training is on their wish list.

When All Is Said And Done

Some of the examples in this chapter apply more specifically to trainers who work for a gym than to trainers who work for themselves, but *ALL* the main principles for closing are the same in either case. You don't really close the sale at the end of a workout. You need to be closing all along. Everything you said and did up until now (even that which preceded the workout like phone calls, emails, and other correspondence) should help seal the deal. The final sale is a formality.

Always be honest with your clients and yourself. In sales, we present the truth in ways intended to help steer customers toward getting what they're looking for (training,) but we should never say anything false. This is very important.

I advise all trainers to memorize their rates. Believe it or not, even though most trainers will tell you that they want more business, an alarming number of them are caught off guard if anyone actually asks what personal training costs. Your chances of executing the sale are far greater when you know the answer.

You can't consider someone your client until they pay you, and they won't remain your client if you do not have a meaningful impact on them. The responsibility is on you. Now that they've signed on, it's your chance to really be a trainer! Shine!

CHAPTER 13

BE TRUE TO YOURSELF

> **"I YAM WHAT I YAM."**
> *–POPEYE THE SAILOR MAN*

ltimately you are selling you. You're selling the experience of being with you. You must believe in the power and value of you, as all successful career trainers do.

Nobody can believe in themselves if they're trying to be someone else. If there is anything in this book that goes against who you are then don't do it.

Diff'rent Strokes

There are more gyms and fitness centers than ever before. They are hiring more trainers every single day. To consumers, working with a trainer is no longer considered to be a luxury. It's the standard. Personal training is the norm, not the exception.

Training is getting more exposure than ever. Celebrity trainers appear everywhere, each with a book, a reality show, and a publicity campaign. With such media overload, we are bombarded with many, often contradicting images of what a personal trainer is. Is it the tough-as-nails drill sergeant from VH-1? Or the hippie I saw on YouTube? Perhaps it's that cheerleader-type from late night infomercials or the tattooed fighter dude in the fitness mag?

Different trainers for different folks.

Just like the TV-show trainers, we professional trainers sometimes fit these caricatures, and there's nothing wrong with that. Find your identity. A soft-spoken guy would sound silly trying to come off as a hard-ass, just as a jock-type would have a tough time acting like a yogi. It's possible to adapt to your client while still being true to yourself. Keep it real is all I'm saying.

I understand that we act as chameleons from time to time, wearing different masks (or hats) for different roles, but when we are true to ourselves, every single mask is still part of the real you.

Be yourself, not what you think a trainer should be. The first trainer of any sort that I was ever aware of was Burgess Meredith's portrayal of Mickey in the classic motion picture *Rocky*. Yet I would sound ridiculous if I screamed "Yer a bum!" at the people I train. Even though Mickey was an awesome character, it's not who I am.

Give great workouts, build strong relationships, sell personal training, and be yourself. In time, you will attract the right clients for you.

THE NINE TYPES OF PERSONAL TRAINERS

DRILL SERGEANT

YOUR TEN REP SET ENDS IN TWENTY REPS.

NICKNAMES: TASK MASTER, SOURPUSS, THE MEAN TRAINER, OL' SNAPPING TURTLE
PROS: GETS RESULTS, HIGH ENERGY
CONS: NOT ALWAYS NICE CLIENTS MAY SHIT THEIR PANTS

OGRE

MAKE SURE YOU HAVE A PROTEIN SHAKE BETWEEN BREAKFAST AND BRUNCH.

NICKNAMES: HUSKY, CHUNK-STYLE, SHREK, BIG GUY(OR GAL)
PROS: APPEARS TO CARE FOR CLIENTS, GENTLE GIANT
CONS: TRAINS EVERYONE TO BULK UP, SPENDS WHOLE PAYCHECK ON FOOD

THE ROOKIE

CAN I OFFER YOU ANOTHER FREE WORKOUT, SIR?

NICKNAMES: NEW JACK CITY, DEER IN THE HEADLIGHTS
PROS: ENTHUSIASTIC, WANTS TO TAKE OVER THE WORLD
CONS: MAY BE UNPREPARED FOR THE HUMBLING THAT AWAITS

NERD

LET'S TRY THIS NEW GADGET I'VE NEVER USED. SOMEONE I DON'T KNOW SAID I SHOULD.

NICKNAMES: CERT JUNKIE, FOUR-EYES, GEARHEAD, MATHMATICIAN
PROS: HAS READ A LOT OF BOOKS, SEEN MANY TUTORIALS, KNOWS NEW TRENDS
CONS: PROBABLY DOESN'T KNOW HOW TO APPLY ANY OF THEM

TOP TRAINER

NOW THAT WE DID AN AMAZING WARM-UP, LET'S HAVE THE BEST WORKOUT EVER, WITH ALL OF YOUR FAVORITE EXERCISES!

NICKNAMES: OL' RELIABLE, THE CLOSER, PROFESSIONAL
PROS: ACTUALLY DOES THEIR JOB, SHOWS UP ON TIME
CONS: MAY REALLY BE DRILL SERGEANT IN DIGUISE

THUG

I DON'T BOX. I FIGHT.

NICKNAMES: THE MACHINE, BEAST, "GET OUTTA MY WAY"
PROS: KNOWS HOW TO TRAIN *AND* HOW TO HUSTLE
CONS: NOT ANYMORE! THESE TRAINERS ALREADY PAID THEIR DEBT TO SOCIETY

JOCK

WHO'S READY FOR SQUAT-THRUSTS?

NICKNAMES: COLLEGE BOY, VARSITY BLUES, JEFFERSON D'ARCEY
PROS: TRAINS EVERYONE LIKE AN ATHLETE
CONS: TRAINS EVERYONE LIKE AN ATHLETE

THE YOGI

OKAY, LET'S SPEND THE SESSION LAYING DOWN AND BREATHING. RELAX.

NICKNAMES: HIPPIE, SURFER, "SQUISHY," CREAM PUFF
PROS: REALLY LAID BACK AND EASY GOING, FUN
CONS: MAY NOT ACTUALLY WORK THEIR CLIENTS OUT

THE FRAUD

HOLD ON A SECOND

NICKNAMES: ZOMBIE (OR ZOMBINA,) OL' TEXTY, "MY ASSHOLE TRAINER"
PROS: NOPE. THESE GUYS ARE AMATEURS.
CONS: WILL NOT SHOW UP ON TIME, GET RESULTS, OR GIVE A SHIT, MAKES US ALL LOOK BAD

DK -13

Respect Your Work, Respect Yourself

In addition to being true to ourselves, we must also be true to the task at hand. Whether you work as a personal trainer or grocery bagger is irrelevant. An individual cannot have self-respect if they do not take pride in their work. So many people accept jobs when they have no intention of doing their best. I never understood that. It makes me sad. Those people would probably be a lot happier if they wanted to do well.

Positivity breeds positivity and doing good work *feels* good! There is no feeling like that of a job well done. I believe the quality of the work one does, even more than the work itself, demonstrates who someone really is (or isn't.) I have more respect for a broke-ass delivery boy who gets his orders out while they're hot, than for a figurehead CEO who inherited a billion-dollar company because of his family ties.

PULL-UPS MAKE YOU STRONG. LIKE MOST THINGS IN LIFE, YOU REAP WHAT YOU SOW.

Beyond Personal Training

The teachings of this book do not only pertain to being a trainer. Although that's our subject, the business practices, DO's & DON'T's, and ways of treating others can be related to learning any new job or skill. From punctuality to honesty. Discipline to follow-through, you can earnestly apply these lessons to just about everything in life. And it's a big, beautiful life...

After dedicating a whole book to advice for job performance, it may appear that I have a "more is more" approach to work, but that's not true. While I'm widely regarded as one of the hardest workers in the game, I feel that none of us should be defined by our careers alone. And while work is extremely important, our family, friends, and loved ones are even more so. As are seeing new places, tasting great food, and experiencing the undiscovered.

"WORKHORSE AND INTERCOURSE."
-TOM WOLFE, FROM THE ELECTRIC
KOOL-AID ACID TEST.

A WORK HARD/FEEL GOOD APPROACH
TO LIFE IS HEALTHY.

I enjoy a Work Hard/Feel Good approach to life. This is healthy. Stress is not. Yes we must put forth great attention and effort to achieve success in any capacity, but let's always keep it in the context of the big picture. I've seen too many trainers burn themselves out. If it ever starts happening to you, then take a break. Call a friend you haven't seen in a while or, even better, go see them. Go somewhere you've never been before, or check out some new music. Try a type of food that you've never had. There is always more to life than your job, even when you love your job, as I do.

Work hard, be yourself, and there will always be a place for your services. So get out there and get paid so you can live life! Everybody needs training! Go get 'em!

...EVEN ME!

FIRST WORKOUT PROTOCOL

> "NO ONE CAN POSSIBLY KNOW WHAT IS ABOUT TO
> HAPPEN: IT IS HAPPENING EACH TIME, FOR THE
> FIRST TIME, FOR THE ONLY TIME."
> -JAMES A. BALDWIN

 ere is a First Workout procedure laid out clearly in ten easy-to-follow steps. These are the guidelines intended to be used along with your instincts and experience.

FWO Procedure Checklist

 1. Call 48 hours in advance. Make note of client's name and any other relevant information. Call again the morning of to confirm/remind. (For appointments before 9am, call again the night before not the morning of.)

2. Alert the front desk of the gym. Tell them you have a new client coming in for the first time who may not be familiar with the club. I do this even at independent training facilities even where the front desk may not know me. If I am meeting a new client at a park or public place, then I get as specific about the location as possible. "Meet me at the northeast corner, Ave B & East 10 St, of Tompkins Square Park, by the jungle gym." Leave nothing to chance.

 3. Shower/brush teeth/wash up. Review any and all notes. Meet the client exactly where you said you would. Be 5 minutes early with a bottle of water and a towel. Smile, shake hands, be friendly, and maintain eye contact. Remind yourself the session is all about them. Use the client's first name.

 4. Continue the questioning process you started with the phone call. Ask the right (open ended) questions. Listen carefully to the answers.

 5. Make your first bold statement (see Chapter 4) based on what the client has been telling you. Warm up and work out your client, while continuing to make bold statements throughout the session: "Wouldn't it feel great if we did this every week?"

 6. Trial Close. Ask if the workout is what they expected. Ask if it exceeds their expectations. Ask if there is anything that they want to work on that you haven't touched upon yet. Gage the workout based on what you see and hear (see Chapter 8.)

7. Ask for the sale early. "Is this something you would like to continue with?" Proceed with the workout while continuing to ask for the sale (see Chapter 12.) Keep painting the big picture. Use words like "we," not "you" as in "If we put in the right effort, there's no way we can fail!"

 8. When they agree to another session, shake hands, high-5, or even hug the client if appropriate. Say "Congratulations! Welcome to the world of personal training!" This will help your new clients commit to one of the best decisions they'll ever make, without you having to use the word "commit."

 9. Start filling out the paperwork for the client. Ask cash or credit. Finalize the sale by taking the cash or swiping the card. Show your enthusiasm for the client, not the sale.

 10. Book the next session.
Look for your next client.

APPENDIX B

SAMPLE WORKOUTS

t's important to know how to train your clients efficiently. Here are some go-to workouts that incorporate active recovery--training multiple muscle groups in succession to maximize time. In other words, while the arms rest, we train the legs. These samples were designed to work the entire body in one session. Most of your clients will not be on a split-routine, which is generally not ideal unless the client trains at least four times a week (a highly unlikely situation.)

I've included three workouts that require minimal or no equipment, with three versions of each depending on your client's fitness level, although there are unlimited possibilities. Repeat each one several times through, with slight variations if appropriate, or mix them up if you prefer. You may want to use the Beginner versions the first time through for your Intermediate clients, or have your Advanced clients do all three versions in a row.

It's a good idea to warm your clients up with a jog, jumping jacks, crawls, or sprints (depending on what they can handle or whatever else you deem appropriate) before the workout.

Remember, these are just examples, intentionally left open to improvisation. I kept them deliberately simple. The basics have been around for so long because they work. Make these workouts your own without being gratuitously flashy. Always be prepared to adjust the intended workout according to what you actually observe taking place in front of you.

The Classic

Also Known As:	Leg/Push/Pull
Required Equipment:	A pull-up bar

Overview: This is one of the most basic strength training circuits around. It is quick and thorough, and can be suited to anyone's needs. As a trainer, you can take your time with it discussing subtlety and technique, or wipe someone out fast, whichever the situation calls for.

Beginner:	Shallow Squats Knee push-ups Trainer-assisted pull-ups
Intermediate:	Deep squats (as low as the client can while maintaining good form) Push-ups Pull-ups
Advanced:	Jump Squats Plyometric push-ups Plyometric pull-ups (or muscle-ups for elite clients)

The Godfather

Also Known As: "All Killer, No Filler"

Required Equipment: A bench or step and pull-up bars. Also barbells, dumbbells, kettle-bells, or medicine balls if available. Use what you got. Bricks and water jugs work too.

Overview: This is about as equipment heavy as I get. Very simple. The blood constantly runs through the body to hit every part hard... especially the heart!

Beginner: Sit down/stand up off bench
Australian (horizontal) pull-ups
Push-ups with hands on bench
Partial bridge
Dips off bench (bent leg)
Lying bent-knee leg raises

Intermediate: Weighted squats
Overhead shoulder press
Pull-ups
Push-ups (on ground, assorted grips—wide, narrow, etc.)
Romanian Deadlifts (barbell or dumbbells)
Dips off of bench (straight leg)
Hanging knee raises

Advanced: Push press (squat and overhead press combined)
Advanced pull-ups (wide grip, mixed grips, plyometric)
Push-ups (hands on dumbbells or medicine balls and/or feet on bench)
Kettlebell swings
Parallel bar dips
Hanging straight-leg raises

The Natural

Also Known As:	Zero Equipment Workout
Required Equipment:	None

Overview: The Natural is beautiful in its simplicity and minimalism. Along with your ability to improvise, this workout really captures the essence of what personal training is all about: You, the trainer, who uses nothing but your knowledge and experience to help your client, who uses nothing but their body. Poetry.

The first three exercises are performed for reps. Planks and handstands should be trained for skill development and practice.

Beginner:	Squats
	Wall push-ups
	Straight bridge (reverse plank)
	Planks

Intermediate:	Split squats
	Diamond-grip (narrow) push-ups
	Back bridge practice
	Front and side planks
	Handstand practice (against wall or trainer assisted)

Advanced:	1-leg squats, 1-leg deadlifts
	1-arm push-ups
	Full back bridge
	1-arm, 1-leg front and side planks
	Handstand push-ups (against wall or trainer assisted if necessary)

YOU,
THE TRAINER,

WHO USES
NOTHING BUT
YOUR
KNOWLEDGE
AND
EXPERIENCE

TO HELP
YOUR CLIENT,

WHO USES
NOTHING BUT
THEIR BODY.

POETRY.

ABOUT THE AUTHOR

Danny Kavadlo is one of the world's most established and respected personal trainers. He has been featured in the New York Times, Men's Fitness, and on television's "20/20".

Danny has worn many hats in the fitness industry. As a personal trainer, he's helped clients of all fitness levels and lifestyles, including athletes, models, celebrities, and everyday professionals. As a fitness manager, he's mentored and developed scores of trainers, directed dozens of corporate seminars, and set sales records which remain unbroken to this day. Hundreds of trainers have successfully employed his methods to increase their client base and salary.

But when all is said and done, Danny is best known as a motivator. Currently, he leads workshops all over the world for fitness professionals and enthusiasts alike. A true in-person experience, Danny is happy to deliver his message and unique training style to the masses.

Danny lives in Brooklyn, NY with his wife Jennifer and son Wilson. Their interests include food, music, and going to the beach.

GRATITUDE

Thanks to my wife, best friend, lover, and soul mate Jennifer Regan-Kavadlo. Babe, we're doin' it! Life is great, and I love you always. I'm so glad we found each other.

To Wilson, I can never fully explain to you how happy and proud you make me every single day, so I'll just say this: Son, you are the best thing that ever happened to me. I am the luckiest man in the world.

Thank you to my parents Rosalie and Carl, who raised me to work hard, show up, and never make excuses. I aspire to be half the parent each one of you has been to me.

To Al, my trainer, my brother, tireless editor, and photographer, I can honestly say this book would not exist without you. LITERALLY. Thank you for motivating me to step up my game. You awakened a part of me that had been sleeping too long. I am grateful.

Jesse, you were my first training partner. Remember Rory's old, dusty weights and the red Dan Lurie body-building book? Or that crappy bench from Consumers and crooked pull-up bar? Thanks for lighting the fire.

Mike Anderson. We've seen a lot, lived a lot, and experienced a lot together. More than most will see in ten lifetimes. I'm glad it was with you, brother.

Thank you Jennie Willink, the best client I ever had and my dear friend. You have no idea how much you've done to help me and my career. I joked for years that all my clients were Six Degrees of Jennie. I am indebted to you. Thank you from the bottom of my heart.

Paul "Coach" Wade, your teachings and experience are a huge part of what's bringing body-weight training back to the masses on a global level. I thank you for that. But on a personal level, you have helped me immensely as a fitness trainer, writer, and teacher. Thank you for spreading the wisdom.

Tremendous thanks to John Du Cane, Adrienne Harvey, Rose Widell, Dennis Armstrong, and the entire crew at Dragon Door. You guys are truly an incredible team and it is a great honor to be associated with you. I look forward to our continued success together.

Derek Brigham, as a fan of your work I was thrilled to hear that you would be involved in this project. Thanks from the bottom of my heart for making my writing look good. You far exceeded my ridiculously high expectations.

Thanks to my esteemed colleague and new best pal, "The Professor" Steven Low for being part of the movement.

Big props to my dudes Josh Murphy, Mike Gibson, and Phil LeDesma at New York Health & Racquet Club. Gentlemen, what can I say? We were the best of the best. Also, thanks to Jeff Bodnar and Randy Humola for the support, encouragement, and opportunities over the years. Some of the best images in this book were shot at NYHRC's flagship 23rd Street location, home to the most excellent personal training staff at any chain gym in NY.

Thank you Rob Severiano, Nate Smith, and Alex Reznik at Complete Body & Spa (19th Street) for giving us free reign to shoot there as well. Rob, you're the man! Thanks for being behind this project 100%. 19th Street is my favorite indoor spot in NYC to train my clients. If you are a trainer and need a great facility, check this place out today.

Thank you, Marvin Ward and James Bertrand from Health & Fitness Annex. For years, I've seen these guys out in the park at 6am while the rest of the city slept. It was a pleasure to photograph them and the incredible participants of their early morning boot camps.

Thanks to Nimble Fitness in Greenwich Village. You guys have always been friends and supporters. New York Times, baby!

Thank you Tony Hamoui, a true class act and one of the best trainers I've ever met, for inspiring the title of this book. I learned a lot from you. Thanks, T! Everybody still needs training... BAD!

Thanks to Buffo, the World's Strongest Clown, for contributing one of my favorite images to Chapter 7. If you get a chance to check out his act, do it! This man is one of a kind and the Kavadlos are huge fans. Learn more at www.Buffo.com

The chart in Chapter 13 is based on the "Life in Hell" comic strips I used to read in the back of the Village Voice when I was ten. Thanks for the inspiration, Matt Groening.

Thank you to all my friends, family, clients, and colleagues. Thanks to the bar and calisthenics community across the world, to my followers and fans, and to "every PCC participant, past and future, who laced up their boots and took on The Century." (Great quote, Coach!) This would not have happened without the inspiration you have given me and I am grateful to you all.

And last, but certainly not least, enormous gratitude to the following health & fitness professionals for making the world a better place every single day. Presented here in alphabetical order by FIRST name, for the trainers: Anthony Johnson, Ammo, Arlene Patruno, Beth Konopka, Carolina Q, Chris Krishna, Christie Miller, Christophe Mendy, Damon Roxas, Dana James "Food Coach,"

Edward Anthony, Eric Bergmann, Errick McAdams, Francisco Alfonseca, Fred Robinson, Fred Wilhelm, Garth Johnson, Hugo German, Jacob Gunther, James Young, Jasmine Brooks, Jason Quick, Jasper Williams, Jeff Monfleury, Jeff Woodard, Joe Vega, Joe Williamson, Johnny Doughtery, Jonathan Blake, Jose Mota, Jose Perez, Joseph DeGeorge, Kalvin Dukes, Kelly Jo Johnson, Kelvin Ali, Kevin Hughes, Krystal Ridgeway, Lenny Addamo, Lincoln Oliver, Marcos Rodriguez, Maria Simone, Raul Robinson, Rex Hughes, Rick Richards, Rob Avelon, Russell Beneke, Ronnie Love, Sean Richmond, Shay from the park, Sheryl Moller at Rocket Nutrition, Steve Ram, Tal, Teddy, Terence Gore, Tony Ebanks, Trainer Steve at KettlebellDaily & Zack Hyman. It is my pleasure to share the training floor with you. Thank you!

Writing a book is like driving cross country or getting a giant tattoo... only longer. You just have to commit and see it through.

Keep the dream alive,

-D. Kavadlo

Al Kavadlo's Progressive Plan for Primal Body Power

What is more satisfying than OWNING a primally powerful, functionally forceful and brute-strong body? A body that packs a punch. A body that commands attention with its etched physique, coiled muscle and proud confidence...A body that can PERFORM at the highest levels of physical accomplishment...

Well, both **Al Kavadlo**—the author of *Pushing the Limits!*—and his brother **Danny**, are supreme testaments to the primal power of body culture done the old-school, ancient way—bare-handed, with your body only. The brothers Kavadlo walk the bodyweight talk—and then some. The proof is evident on every page of *Pushing the Limits!*

Your body is your temple. Protect and strengthen your temple by modeling the methods of the exercise masters. Al Kavadlo has modeled the masters and has the "temple" to show for it. Follow Al's progressive plan for primal body power within the pages of *Pushing the Limits!*—follow in the footsteps of the great bodyweight exercise masters—and you too can build the explosive strength and possess the magnificent physique you deserve.

"When people ask me about bodyweight strength training, I point them to Al Kavadlo. *Pushing the Limits!* is a must-have for bodyweight training enthusiasts or anyone looking to build strength without lifting weights. Al lays out dozens of effective exercises for every fitness level, while making the journey fun and encouraging."—**MARK SISSON**, author of *The Primal Blueprint*

"In this awesome new book, Al only asks that you find ONE piece of equipment—your body! Stoic, Spartan, perfection...this book is bodyweight strength training for the ultimate purist!"—**PAUL WADE**, author of *Convict Conditioning*

"This is the book I wish I had when I first started working out. Knowing Al's secrets and various progressions would have saved me years of wasted time, frustration and injuries. The variations of The Big Three and progressions Al lays out will keep you busy for years."—**JASON FERRUGGIA**

"Whether you are an advanced bodyweight conditioning athlete or a wet behind the ears newbie, Al's *Pushing the Limits!* has something for you. Easy to follow progressions allow you to master advanced push up, squat and bridging variations. All you need is the will to do it! No gym required."
—**ROBB WOLF**, author of *The Paleo Solution*

"I LOVE this freaking Book!!! Every time you put out a new book it becomes my NEW favorite and my inspiration! I love the blend of strength, power, health and overall athleticism in this book! This book covers the BIG picture of training for ALL aspects of human performance.

I will use it with my athletes, with the adults I train, in my own training and absolutely these books will be the books I share with my kids. This stuff reminds me of the old school Strength & Health Magazine, I'm fired UP!"—**ZACH EVEN-ESH**, author of *Bodyweight Bodybuilding Training System*

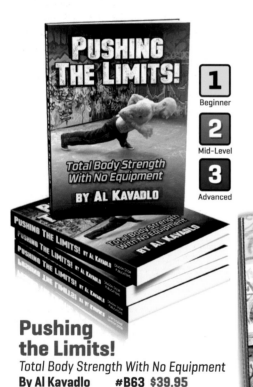

Pushing the Limits!
Total Body Strength With No Equipment
By Al Kavadlo　#B63　$39.95
224 pages, 330 Photos

1	Beginner
2	Mid-Level
3	Advanced

Go Beyond Mere "Toughness"— When You Master The Art of Bar Athletics and Sculpt the Ultimate in Upper Body Physiques

Raising the Bar
The Definitive Guide to Bar Calisthenics
By Al Kavadlo **#B63 $39.95**
224 pages, 330 Photos

[1] Beginner [2] Mid-Level [3] Advanced

Raising the Bar breaks down every type of exercise you can do with a pull-up bar. From the basic two arm hang, to the mighty muscle-up, all the way to the elusive one arm pull-up, "bar master" Al Kavadlo takes you step by expert step through everything you need to do to build the chiseled frame you've always wanted.

Whether you're a die-hard calisthenics enthusiast or just looking to get in the best shape of your life, *Raising the Bar* will meet all your expectations—and then some!

The message is clear: you can earn yourself a stunning upper body with just 3 basic moves and 1 super-simple, yet amazingly versatile tool.

And what's even better, this 3 + 1 formula for upper body magnificence hides enough variety to keep you challenged and surging to new heights for a lifetime of cool moves and ever-tougher progressions!

Cast in the "concrete jungle" of urban scaffolding and graffiti-laden, blasted walls—and sourced from iconic bar-athlete destinations like Tompkins Square Park, NYC—*Raising the Bar* rears up to grab you by the throat and hurl you into an inspiring new vision of what the human body can achieve. Embrace Al Kavadlo's vision, pick up the challenge, share the Quest, follow directions—and the Holy Grail of supreme upper body fitness is yours for the taking.

A Kick Ass Encyclopedia of Bodyweight Exercises

How Do YOU Stack Up Against These 6 Signs of a TRUE Physical Specimen?

According to Paul Wade's *Convict Conditioning* you earn the right to call yourself a "true physical specimen" if you can perform the following:

✔ 1. AT LEAST one set of 5 one-arm pushups each side— with the ELITE goal of 100 sets each side

✔ 2. AT LEAST one set of 5 one-leg squats each side— with the ELITE goal of 2 sets of 50 each side

✔ 3. AT LEAST a single one-arm pullup each side— with the ELITE goal of 2 sets of 6 each side

✔ 4. AT LEAST one set of 5 hanging straight leg raises— with the ELITE goal of 2 sets of 30

✔ 5. AT LEAST one stand-to-stand bridge— with the ELITE goal of 2 sets of 30

✔ 6. AT LEAST a single one-arm handstand pushup on each side— with the ELITE goal of 1 set of 5

Well, how DO you stack up?

Chances are that whatever athletic level you have achieved, there are some serious gaps in your OVERALL strength program. Gaps that stop you short of being able to claim status as a truly accomplished strength athlete.

The good news is that—in *Convict Conditioning*—Paul Wade has laid out a brilliant 6-set system of 10 progressions which allows you to master these elite levels.

And you could be starting at almost any age and in almost in any condition...

Paul Wade has given you the keys—ALL the keys you'll ever need— that will open door, after door, after door for you in your quest for supreme physical excellence. Yes, it will be the hardest work you'll ever have to do. And yes, 97% of those who pick up *Convict Conditioning*, frankly, won't have the guts and the fortitude to make it. But if you make it even half-way through **Paul's Progressions**, you'll be stronger than almost anyone you encounter. Ever.

Here's just a small taste of what you'll get with *Convict Conditioning*:

Can you meet these 5 benchmarks of the *truly* powerful?... Page 1

The nature and the art of real strength... Page 2

Why mastery of *progressive calisthenics* is the ultimate secret for building maximum raw strength... Page 2

A dozen one-arm handstand pushups without support— anyone? Anyone?... Page 3

How to rank in a powerlifting championship—*without ever training with weights*... Page 4

Calisthenics as a hardcore strength training technology... Page 9

Spartan "300" calisthenics at the Battle of Thermopolylae... Page 10

How to cultivate the perfect body—the Greek and Roman way... Page 10

The difference between "old school" and "new school" calisthenics... Page 15

The role of prisons in preserving the older systems... Page 16

Strength training as a primary survival strategy... Page 16

The 6 basic benefits of bodyweight training... Pages 22—27

Why calisthenics are the *ultimate* in functional training... Page 23

The value of cultivating *self-movement*—rather than *object-movement*... Page 23

The *real* source of strength—it's not your *muscles*... Page 24

One crucial reason why a lot of convicts deliberately avoid weight-training... Page 24

How to progressively strengthen your joints over a lifetime—and even heal old joint injuries... Page 25

Why "authentic" exercises like pullups are so perfect for strength and power development... Page 25

Bodyweight training for quick physique perfection... Page 26

How to normalize and regulate your body fat levels—with bodyweight training only... Page 27

Why weight-training and the psychology of overeating go hand in hand... Page 27

The best approach for rapidly strengthening your whole body is this... Page 30

This is the most important and revolutionary feature of *Convict Conditioning*.... Page 33

A jealously-guarded system for going from puny to powerful— when your life may depend on the speed of your results... Page 33

The 6 "Ultimate" Master Steps—only a handful of athletes in the whole world can correctly perform them all. Can you?... Page 33

How to Forge Armor-Plated Pecs and Steel Triceps... Page 41

Why the pushup is the *ultimate* upper body exercise—and better than the bench press... Page 41

How to effectively bulletproof the vulnerable rotator cuff muscles... Page 42

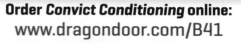

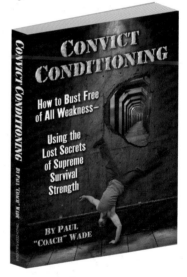

1 Beginner 2 Mid-Level 3 Advanced

Convict Conditioning

How to Bust Free of All Weakness—Using the Lost Secrets of Supreme Survival Strength

By Paul "Coach" Wade
#B41 $39.95

Paperback 8.5 x 11 320 pages
191 photos, charts and illustrations

Dragon Door Customer Acclaim for Paul Wade's *Convict Conditioning*

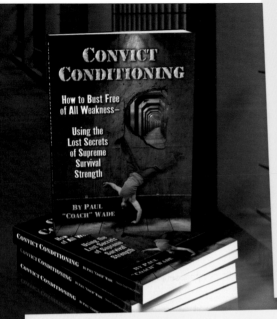

A Strength Training Guide That Will Never Be Duplicated!

"I knew within the first chapter of reading this book that I was in for something special and unique. The last time I felt this same feeling was when reading *Power to the People!* To me this is the Body Weight equivalent to Pavel's masterpiece.

Books like this can never be duplicated. Paul Wade went through a unique set of circumstances of doing time in prison with an 'old time' master of calisthenics. Paul took these lessons from this 70 year old strong man and mastered them over a period of 20 years while 'doing time'. He then taught these methods to countless prisoners and honed his teaching to perfection.

I believe that extreme circumstances like this are what it takes to create a true masterpiece. I know that 'masterpiece' is a strong word, but this is as close as it gets. No other body weight book I have read (and I have a huge fitness library)...comes close to this as far as gaining incredible strength from body weight exercise.

Just like Power to the People, I am sure I will read this over and over again...mastering the principles that Paul Wade took 20 years to master.

Outstanding Book!"—*Rusty Moore - Fitness Black Book - Seattle, WA*

A must for all martial artists

"As a dedicated martial artist for more than seven years, this book is exactly what I've been looking for.

For a while now I have trained with machines at my local gym to improve my muscle strength and power and get to the next level in my training. I always felt that the modern health club, technology based exercise jarred with my martial art though, which only required body movement.

Finally this book has come along. At last I can combine perfect body movement for martial skill with perfect body exercise for ultimate strength.

All fighting arts are based on body movement. This book is a complete textbook on how to max out your musclepower using only body movement, as different from dumbbells, machines or gadgets. For this reason it belongs on the bookshelf of every serious martial artist, male and female, young and old."—*Gino Cartier - Washington DC*

I've packed all of my other training books away!

"I read CC in one go. I couldn't put it down. I have purchased a lot of bodyweight training books in the past, and have always been pretty disappointed. They all seem to just have pictures of different exercises, and no plan whatsoever on how to implement them and progress with them. But not with this one. The information in this book is AWESOME! I like to have a clear, logical plan of progression to follow, and that is what this book gives. I have put all of my other training books away. CC is the only system I am going to follow. This is now my favorite training book ever!"—*Lyndan - Australia*

Brutal Elegance.

"I have been training and reading about training since I first joined the US Navy in the 1960s. I thought I'd seen everything the fitness world had to offer. Sometimes twice. But I was wrong. This book is utterly iconoclastic.

The author breaks down all conceivable body weight exercises into six basic movements, each designed to stimulate different vectors of the muscular system. These six are then elegantly and very intelligently broken into ten progressive techniques. You master one technique, and move on to the next.

The simplicity of this method belies a very powerful and complex training paradigm, reduced into an abstraction that obviously took many years of sweat and toil to develop.

Trust me. Nobody else worked this out. This approach is completely unique and fresh.

I have read virtually every calisthenics book printed in America over the last 40 years, and instruction like this can't be found anywhere, in any one of them. *Convict Conditioning* is head and shoulders above them all. In years to come, trainers and coaches will all be talking about 'progressions' and 'progressive calisthenics' and claim they've been doing it all along. But the truth is that Dragon Door bought it to you first. As with kettlebells, they were the trail blazers.

Who should purchase this volume? Everyone who craves fitness and strength should. Even if you don't plan to follow the routines, the book will make you think about your physical prowess, and will give even world class experts food for thought. At the very least if you find yourself on vacation or away on business without your barbells, this book will turn your hotel into a fully equipped gym.

I'd advise any athlete to obtain this work as soon as possible."—*Bill Oliver - Albany, NY, United States*

More Dragon Door Customer Acclaim for *Convict Conditioning*

Fascinating Reading and Real Strength

"Coach Wade's system is a real eye opener if you've been a lifetime iron junkie. Wanna find out how really strong (or weak) you are? Get this book and begin working through the 10 levels of the 6 power exercises. I was pleasantly surprised by my ability on a few of the exercises...but some are downright humbling. If I were on a desert island with only one book on strength and conditioning this would be it. (Could I staple Pavel's "Naked Warrior" to the back and count them as one???!) Thanks Dragon Door for this innovative new author."—*Jon Schultheis, RKC (2005) - Keansburg, NJ*

Single best strength training book ever!

"I just turned 50 this year and I have tried a little bit of everything over the years: martial arts, swimming, soccer, cycling, free weights, weight machines, even yoga and Pilates. I started using *Convict Conditioning* right after it came out. I started from the beginning, like Coach Wade says, doing mostly step one or two for five out of the six exercises. I work out 3 to 5 times a week, usually for 30 to 45 minutes.

Long story short, my weight went up 14 pounds (I was not trying to gain weight) but my body fat percentage dropped two percent. That translates into approximately 19 pounds of lean muscle gained in two months! I've never gotten this kind of results with anything else I've ever done. Now I have pretty much stopped lifting weights for strength training. Instead, I lift once a week as a test to see how much stronger I'm getting without weight training. There are a lot of great strength training books in the world (most of them published by Dragon Door), but if I had to choose just one, this is the single best strength training book ever. BUY THIS BOOK. FOLLOW THE PLAN. GET AS STRONG AS YOU WANT. "—*Wayne - Decatur, GA*

Best bodyweight training book so far!

"I'm a martial artist and I've been training for years with a combination of weights and bodyweight training and had good results from both (but had the usual injuries from weight training). I prefer the bodyweight stuff though as it trains me to use my whole body as a unit, much more than weights do, and I notice the difference on the mat and in the ring. Since reading this book I have given the weights a break and focused purely on the bodyweight exercise progressions as described by 'Coach' Wade and my strength had increased more than ever before. So far I've built up to 12 strict one-leg squats each leg and 5 uneven pull ups each arm.

I've never achieved this kind of strength before - and this stuff builds solid muscle mass as well. It's very intense training. I am so confident in and happy with the results I'm getting that I've decided to train for a fitness/bodybuilding comp just using his techniques, no weights, just to show for real what kind of a physique these exercises can build. In sum, I cannot recommend 'Coach' Wade's book highly enough - it is by far the best of its kind ever!"—*Mark Robinson - Australia, currently living in South Korea*

A lifetime of lifting...and continued learning.

"I have been working out diligently since 1988 and played sports in high school and college before that. My stint the Army saw me doing calisthenics, running, conditioning courses, forced marches, etc. There are many levels of strength and fitness. I have been as big as 240 in my powerlifting/strongman days and as low as 185-190 while in the Army. I think I have tried everything under the sun: the high intensity of Arthur Jones and Dr. Ken, the Super Slow of El Darden, and the brutality of Dinosaur Training Brooks Kubic made famous.

This is one of the BEST books I've ever read on real strength training which also covers other just as important aspects of health; like staying injury free, feeling healthy and becoming flexible. It's an excellent book. He tells you the why and the how with his progressive plan. This book is a GOLD MINE and worth 100 times what I paid for it!"
—*Horst - Woburn, MA*

This book sets the standard, ladies and gentlemen

"It's difficult to describe just how much this book means to me. I've been training hard since I was in the RAF nearly ten years ago, and to say this book is a breakthrough is an understatement. How often do you really read something so new, so fresh? This book contains a complete new system of calisthenics drawn from American prison training methods. When I say 'system' I mean it. It's complete (rank beginner to expert), it's comprehensive (all the exercises and photos are here), it's graded (progressions from exercise to exercise are smooth and pre-determined) and it's totally original. Whether you love or hate the author, you have to listen to him. And you will learn something. This book just makes SENSE. In twenty years people will still be buying it."—Andy McMann - Ponty, Wales, GB

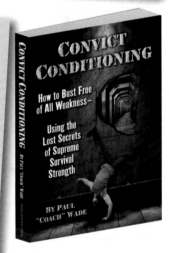

Convict Conditioning
How to Bust Free of All Weakness—Using the Lost Secrets of Supreme Survival Strength
By Paul "Coach" Wade
#B41 $39.95
Paperback 8.5 x 11 320 pages
191 photos, charts and illustrations

1 Beginner **2** Mid-Level **3** Advanced

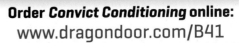

The Experts Give High Praise to
Convict Conditioning 2

"Coach Paul Wade has outdone himself. His first book *Convict Conditioning* is to my mind THE BEST book ever written on bodyweight conditioning. Hands down. Now, with the sequel *Convict Conditioning 2*, Coach Wade takes us even deeper into the subtle nuances of training with the ultimate resistance tool: our bodies.

In plain English, but with an amazing understanding of anatomy, physiology, kinesiology and, go figure, psychology, Coach Wade explains very simply how to work the smaller but just as important areas of the body such as the hands and forearms, neck and calves and obliques in serious functional ways.

His minimalist approach to exercise belies the complexity of his system and the deep insight into exactly how the body works and the best way to get from A to Z in the shortest time possible.

I got the best advice on how to strengthen the hard-to-reach extensors of the hand right away from this exercise Master I have ever seen. It's so simple but so completely functional I can't believe no one else has thought of it yet. Just glad he figured it out for me.

Paul teaches us how to strengthen our bodies with the simplest of movements while at the same time balancing our structures in the same way: simple exercises that work the whole body.

And just as simply as he did with his first book. His novel approach to stretching and mobility training is brilliant and fresh as well as his take on recovery and healing from injury. Sprinkled throughout the entire book are too-many-to-count insights and advice from a man who has come to his knowledge the hard way and knows exactly of what he speaks.

This book is, as was his first, an amazing journey into the history of physical culture disguised as a book on calisthenics. But the thing that Coach Wade does better than any before him is his unbelievable progressions on EVERY EXERCISE and stretch! He breaks things down and tells us EXACTLY how to proceed to get to whatever level of strength and development we want. AND gives us the exact metrics we need to know when to go to the next level.

Adding in completely practical and immediately useful insights into nutrition and the mindset necessary to deal not only with training but with life, makes this book a classic that will stand the test of time.

Bravo Coach Wade, Bravo." —**Mark Reifkind, Master RKC,** author of *Mastering the HardStyle Kettlebell Swing*

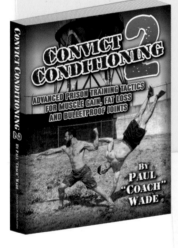

Convict Conditioning 2
Advanced Prison Training Tactics for Muscle Gain, Fat Loss and Bulletproof Joints
By Paul "Coach" Wade
#B59 **$39.95**
Paperback 8.5 x 11 354 pages
261 photos, charts and illustrations

2 Mid-Level

3 Advanced

"The overriding principle of *Convict Conditioning 2* is 'little equipment-big rewards'. For the athlete in the throwing and fighting arts, the section on Lateral Chain Training, Capturing the Flag, is a unique and perhaps singular approach to training the obliques and the whole family of side muscles. This section stood out to me as ground breaking and well worth the time and energy by anyone to review and attempt to complete. Literally, this is a new approach to lateral chain training that is well beyond sidebends and suitcase deadlifts.

The author's review of passive stretching reflects the experience of many of us in the field. But, his solution might be the reason I am going to recommend this work for everyone: The Trifecta. This section covers what the author calls The Functional Triad and gives a series of simple progressions to three holds that promise to oil your joints. It's yoga for the strength athlete and supports the material one would find, for example, in Pavel's *Loaded Stretching*.

I didn't expect to like this book, but I come away from it practically insisting that everyone read it. It is a strongman book mixed with yoga mixed with street smarts. I wanted to hate it, but I love it."
—**Dan John,** author of *Don't Let Go* and co-author of *Easy Strength*

"I've been lifting weights for over 50 years and have trained in the martial arts since 1965. I've read voraciously on both subjects, and written dozens of magazine articles and many books on the subjects. This book and Wade's first, *Convict Conditioning*, are by far the most commonsense, information-packed, and result producing I've read. These books will truly change your life.

Paul Wade is a new and powerful voice in the strength and fitness arena, one that is commonsense, inspiring, and in your face. His approach to maximizing your body's potential is not the same old hackneyed material you find in every book and magazine piece that pictures steroid-bloated models screaming as they curl weights. Wade's stuff has been proven effective by hard men who don't tolerate fluff. It will work for you, too—guaranteed.

As an ex-cop, I've gone mano-y-mano with ex-cons that had clearly trained as Paul Wade suggests in his two *Convict Conditioning* books. While these guys didn't look like steroid-fueled bodybuilders (actually, there were a couple who did), all were incredibly lean, hard and powerful. Wade blows many commonly held beliefs about conditioning, strengthening, and eating out of the water and replaces them with result-producing information that won't cost you a dime." —**Loren W. Christensen,** author of *Fighting the Pain Resistant Attacker,* and many other titles

"*Convict Conditioning* is one of the most influential books I ever got my hands on. *Convict Conditioning 2* took my training and outlook on the power of bodyweight training to the 10th degree—from strengthening the smallest muscles in a maximal manner, all the way to using bodyweight training as a means of healing injuries that pile up from over 22 years of aggressive lifting.

I've used both *Convict Conditioning* and *Convict Conditioning 2* on myself and with my athletes. Without either of these books I can easily say that these boys would not be the BEASTS they are today. Without a doubt *Convict Conditioning 2* will blow you away and inspire and educate you to take bodyweight training to a whole NEW level."
—**Zach Even-Esh,** Underground Strength Coach

—TABLE OF CONTENTS—

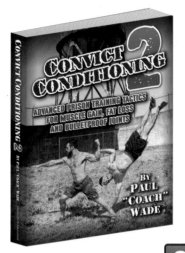

Convict Conditioning 2

Advanced Prison Training Tactics for Muscle Gain, Fat Loss and Bulletproof Joints

By Paul "Coach" Wade

#B59 $39.95

Paperback 8.5 x 11   354 pages
261 photos, charts and illustrations

2 Mid-Level
3 Advanced

GET DYNAMIC, CHISELLED, POWER-JACK LEGS AND DEVELOP EXPLOSIVE LOWER-BODY STRENGTH— WITH PAUL "COACH" WADE'S ULTIMATE
BODYWEIGHT SQUAT COURSE

Paul Wade's *Convict Conditioning Ultimate Bodyweight Squat Course* explodes out of the cellblock to teach you in absolute detail how to progress from the ease of a simple shoulderstand squat—to the stunning "1-in-10,000" achievement of the prison-style one-leg squat. Ten progressive steps guide you to bodyweight squat mastery. Do it—and become a Bodyweight Squat Immortal.

This home-study course in ultimate survival strength comes replete with bonus material not available in **Paul Wade's** original *Convict Conditioning* book—and numerous key training tips that refine and expand on the original program.

A heavily and gorgeously-illustrated 80-plus-page manual gives you the entire film script to study at your leisure, with brilliant, precise photographs to remind you of the essential movements you absorbed in the DVD itself.

Paul Wade adds a bonus **Ten Commandments for Perfect Bodyweight Squats**—which is worth the price of admission alone. And there's the additional bonus of **5 major Variant drill**s to add explosivity, fun and super-strength to your core practice.

Whatever you are looking for from your bodyweight squats— be it supreme functional strength, monstrous muscle growth or explosive leg power—it's yours for the progressive taking with *Convict Conditioning, Volume 2: The Ultimate Bodyweight Squat Course.*

WHY EVERY SELF-RESPECTING MAN WILL BE RELIGIOUS ABOUT HIS SQUATS...

Leg training is vital for every athlete. A well-trained, muscular upper body teetering around on skinny stick legs is a joke. Don't be that joke! The mighty squat is the answer to your prayers. Here's why:

- Squats train virtually every muscle in the lower body, from quads and glutes to hips, lower back and even hamstrings.

- Squat deep—as we'll teach you—and you will seriously increase your flexibility and ankle strength.

- All functional power is transmitted through the legs, so without strong, powerful legs you are *nothing*—that goes for running, jumping and combat sports as much as it does for lifting heavy stuff.

ARE YOU FAILING TO BUILD MONSTROUS LEGS FROM SQUATS—BECAUSE OF THESE MISTAKES?

Most trainees learn how to squat on two legs, and then make the exercise harder by slapping a barbell across their back. In prison, this way of adding strength wasn't always available, so cell trainees developed ways of progressing using only bodyweight versus gravity. The best way to do this is to learn how to squat all the way down to the ground and back up on just one leg.

Not everybody who explores prison training will have the dedication and drive to achieve strength feats like the one-arm pullup, but the legs are much stronger than the arms. If you put in the time and work hard, the one-leg squat will be within the reach of almost every athlete who pays their dues.

But the one-leg squat still requires very powerful muscles and tendons, so you don't want to jump into one-leg squatting right away. You need to build the joint strength and muscle to safely attempt this great exercise. Discover how to do that safely, using ten steps, ten progressively harder squat exercises.

IN THE STRENGTH GAME, FOOLS RUSH IN WHERE ANGELS FEAR TO TREAD

The wise old Chinese man shouted to his rickshaw driver: "Slow down, young man, I'm in a hurry!" If ever a warning needed to be shouted to our nation of compulsive strength-addicts, this would be it. You see them everywhere: the halt, the lame, the jacked-up, the torn, the pain-ridden—the former glory-seekers who have been reduced to sad husks of their former selves by rushing helter-skelter into heavy lifting without having first built a firm foundation.

Paul Wade reveals the ten key points of perfect squat form. The aspects of proper form apply to all your squats, and they'll not only unlock the muscle and power-building potential of each rep you do, but they'll also keep you as safe as you can be.

Bodyweight training is all about improving strength and health, not building up a list of injuries or aches and pains. They are so fundamental, we call them the Ten Commandments of good squat form.

Obey the Ten Commandments, follow the brilliantly laid out progressions religiously and you simply CANNOT fail to get stronger and stronger and stronger and stronger and stronger—surely, safely and for as long as you live...

COMPLEX MADE SIMPLE

Having read both *Convict Conditioning* and *Convict Conditioning 2*, the complementary DVD series is an excellent translation of the big six movement progressions into a simple to follow DVD. The demonstration of movement progression through the 10 levels is well described and easy to follow.

As a Physical Therapist it is a very useful way to teach safe progressions to patients/clients and other professionals. I have already used Volume I (the push up progression) to teach high school strength coaches how to safely progress athletes with pressing activity and look forward to using volume 2 with these same coaches. I think anyone who studies movement realizes very few athletes can properly squat with two legs, let alone one.

You will not find an easier way to teach the squat. Well done again Paul. Look forward to the rest of the series."

—Andrew Marchesi PT/MPT, FAFS, Scottsdale, AZ

Convict Conditioning
Volume 2: The Ultimate Bodyweight Squat Course
By Paul "Coach" Wade featuring Brett Jones and Max Shank
#DV084 $69.95
DVD 56 minutes with full color Companion Manual, 88 pages

1 Beginner

2 Mid-Level

3 Advanced

NAVY SEAL ON THE ROAD

"My whole team uses it. We can work out effectively anywhere and I mean anywhere!"
—Tyler Archer, Navy

GET A ROCK-HARD, BRUTISHLY POWERFUL UPPER FRAME AND ACHIEVE ELITE-LEVEL STRENGTH— WITH PAUL "COACH" WADE'S PRISON-STYLE PUSHUP PROGRAM

Paul Wade's *Convict Conditioning* system represents the ultimate distillation of hardcore prison bodyweight training's most powerful methods. What works was kept. What didn't, was slashed away. When your life is on the line, you're not going to mess with less than the absolute best. Many of these older, very potent solitary training systems have been on the verge of dying, as convicts begin to gain access to weights, and modern "bodybuilding thinking" floods into the prisons.

Thanks to Paul Wade, these ultimate strength survival secrets have been saved for posterity. And for you...

Filmed entirely—and so appropriately—on "The Rock", Wade's *Convict Conditioning Prison Pushup Series* explodes out of the cellblock to teach you in absolute detail how to progress from the ease of a simple wall pushup—to the stunning "1-in-10,000" achieve-

ment of the prison-style one-arm pushup. Ten progressive steps guide you to pushup mastery. Do it—and become a Pushup God.

This home-study course in ultimate survival strength comes replete with bonus material not available in **Paul Wade's** original *Convict Conditioning* book—and numerous key training tips that refine and expand on the original program.

A heavily and gorgeously-illustrated 80-plus-page manual gives you the entire film script to study at your leisure, with brilliant, precise photographs to remind you of the essential movements you absorbed in the DVD itself.

Paul Wade adds a bonus **Ten Commandments for Perfect Pushups**—which is worth the price of admission alone. And there's the additional bonus of **5 major Variant drills** to add explosivity, fun and super-strength to your core practice.

Whatever you are looking for from your pushups—be it supreme functional strength, monstrous muscle growth or explosive upper-body power—it's yours for the progressive taking with *Convict Conditioning, Volume 1: The Prison Pushup Series*.

1 Beginner

2 Mid-Level

3 Advanced

Convict Conditioning
Volume 1: The Prison Pushup Series
By Paul "Coach" Wade featuring Brett Jones and Max Shank
#DV083 $69.95
DVD 59 minutes with full color Companion Manual, 88 pages

DEMONIC ABS ARE A MAN'S BEST FRIEND—DISCOVER HOW TO SEIZE A SIX-PACK FROM HELL AND OWN THE WORLD... LEG RAISES

Paul Wade's *Convict Conditioning 3, Leg Raises: Six Pack from Hell* teaches you in absolute detail how to progress from the ease of a simple Knee Tuck—to the magnificent, "1-in-1,000" achievement of the Hanging Straight Leg Raise. Ten progressive steps guide you to inevitable mastery of this ultimate abs exercise. Do it, seize the knowledge—but beware—the Gods will be jealous!

This home-study course in ultimate survival strength comes replete with bonus material not available in **Paul Wade's** original *Convict Conditioning* book—and numerous key training tips that refine and expand on the original program.

Prowl through the heavily and gorgeously-illustrated 80-plus-page manual and devour the entire film script at your animal leisure. Digest the brilliant, precise photographs and reinforce the raw benefits you absorbed from the DVD.

Paul Wade adds a bonus **Ten Commandments for Perfect Bodyweight Squats**—which is worth the price of admission alone. And there's the additional bonus of **4 major Variant drills** to add explosivity, fun and super-strength to your core practice.

Whatever you are looking for when murdering your abs—be it a fist-breaking, rock-like shield of impenetrable muscle, an uglier-is-more-beautiful set of rippling abdominal ridges, or a monstrous injection of lifting power—it's yours for the progressive taking with *Convict Conditioning, Volume 3, Leg Raises: Six Pack from Hell*

PRISON-STYLE MIDSECTION TRAINING— FOR AN ALL SHOW AND ALL GO PHYSIQUE

When convicts train their waists, they want real, noticeable results—and by "results" we don't mean that they want cute, tight little defined abs. We mean that they want thick, strong, muscular midsections. They want *functionally* powerful abs and hips they can use for heavy lifting, kicking, and brawling. They want guts so strong from their training that it actually hurts an attacker to punch them in the belly. Prison abs aren't about all show, no go—a prison-built physique has to be all show and all go. Those guys don't just want six-packs—they want six-packs from Hell.

And, for the first time, we're going to show you how these guys get what they want. We're not going to be using sissy machines or easy isolation exercises—we're going straight for the old school secret weapon for gut training; progressive leg raises.

If you want a six-pack from Hell, the first thing you need to do is focus your efforts. If a weightlifter wanted a very thick, powerful chest in a hurry, he wouldn't spread his efforts out over a dozen exercises and perform them gently all day long. No—he'd pick just one exercise, probably the bench press, and just focus on getting stronger and stronger on that lift until he was monstrously strong. When he reached this level, and his pecs were thick slabs of meat, only then would he maybe begin sculpting them with minor exercises and higher reps.

It's no different if you want a mind-blowing midsection. Just pick one exercise that hits all the muscles in the midsection—the hip flexors, the abs, the intercostals, the obliques—then blast it.

And the one exercise we're going to discover is the best midsection exercise known to man, and the most popular amongst soldiers, warriors, martial artists and prison athletes since men started working out—the leg raise.

You'll discover ten different leg raise movements, each one a little harder than the last. You'll learn how to get the most out of each of these techniques, each of these ten steps, before moving up to the next step. By the time you get through all ten steps and you're working with the final Master Step of the leg raise series, you'll have a solid, athletic, stomach made of steel, as well as powerful hips and a ribcage armored with dense muscle. You'll have abs that would've made Bruce Lee take notice!

THE TEN COMMANDMENTS YOU MUST OBEY TO EARN A REAL MONSTER OF AN ATHLETIC CORE

Paul Wade gives you ten key points, the "Ten Commandments" of leg raises, that will take your prison-style core training from just "okay" to absolutely phenomenal. We want the results to be so effective that they'll literally shock you. This kind of accelerated progress can be achieved, but if you want to achieve it you better listen carefully to these ten key pointers you'll discover with the DVD.

Bodyweight mastery is a lot like high-level martial arts. It's more about *principles* than individual techniques. Really study and absorb these principles, and you'll be on your way to a six-pack from Hell in no time.

The hanging straight leg raise, performed strictly and for reps, is the Gold Standard of abdominal strength techniques. Once you're at the level where you can throw out sets of twenty to thirty rock solid reps of this exercise, your abs will be thick and strong, but more importantly, they'll be functional—not just a pretty six-

pack, but a real monster of an athletic core, which is capable of developing high levels of force.

Hanging will work your serratus and intercostals, making these muscles stand out like fingers, and your obliques and flank muscles will be tight and strong from holding your hips in place. Your lumbar spine will achieve a gymnastic level of flexibility, like fluid steel, and your chances of back pain will be greatly reduced.

The bottom line: If you want to be stronger and more athletic than the next guy, you need the edge that straight leg raises can give you.

ERECT TWIN PYTHONS OF COILED BEEF UP YOUR SPINE AND DEVELOP EXTREME, EXPLOSIVE RESILIENCE—WITH THE DYNAMIC POWER AND FLEXIBLE STRENGTH OF ADVANCED BRIDGING

Paul Wade's *Convict Conditioning* system represents the ultimate distillation of hardcore prison bodyweight training's most powerful methods. What works was kept. What didn't, was slashed away. When your life is on the line, you're not going to mess with less than the absolute best. Many of these older, very potent solitary training systems have been on the verge of dying, as convicts begin to gain access to weights, and modern "bodybuilding thinking" floods into the prisons. Thanks to Paul Wade, these ultimate strength survival secrets have been saved for posterity. And for you...

Filmed entirely—and so appropriately— on "The Rock", Wade's *Convict Conditioning Volume 4, Advanced Bridging: Forging an Iron Spine* explodes out of the cellblock to teach you in absolute detail how to progress from the relative ease of a Short Bridge—to the stunning, "1-in-1,000" achievement of the Stand-to-Stand Bridge. Ten progressive steps guide you to inevitable mastery of this ultimate exercise for an unbreakable back.

This home-study course in ultimate survival strength comes replete with bonus material not available in **Paul Wade's** original *Convict Conditioning* book—and numerous key training tips that refine and expand on the original program.

Prowl through the heavily and gorgeously-illustrated 80-plus-page manual and devour the entire film script at your animal leisure. Digest the brilliant, precise photographs and reinforce the raw benefits you absorbed from the DVD.

Paul Wade adds a bonus **Ten Commandments for Perfect Bridges**—which is worth the price of admission alone. And there's the additional bonus of **4 major Variant drills** to add explosivity, fun and super-strength to your core practice.

Whatever you are looking for from your pushups—be it supreme functional strength, monstrous muscle growth or explosive upper-body power—it's yours for the progressive taking with *Convict Conditioning Volume 4: Advanced Bridging: Forging an Iron Spine.*

FILMED ENTIRELY AT ALCATRAZ ON LOCATION AT

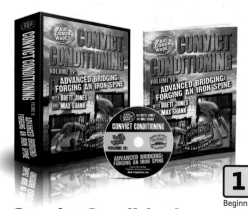

Convict Conditioning
Volume 4: Advanced Bridging: Forging an Iron Spine
By Paul "Coach" Wade featuring Brett Jones and Max Shank
#DV087 $59.95
DVD 59 minutes with full color Companion Manual, 88 pages

1 Beginner
2 Mid-Level
3 Advanced

Build Your Body To Be Ripped, Rugged and Spectacular—With Dragon Door's Best-of-Class, RKC Kettlebell

The Ultimate "Handheld Gym"— Designed for A Lifetime of Hard, High-Performance Use...

Even a man of average initial strength can immediately start using the 16kg/35lb kettlebell for two-handed swings and quickly gravitate to one-handed swings, followed by jerks, cleans and snatches. Within a few weeks you can expect to see spectacular gains in overall strength and conditioning—and for many—significant fat loss.

Dragon Door re-introduced kettlebells to the US with the uniquely designed 35lb cast iron kettlebell—and it has remained our most popular kettlebell. Why? Let Dragon Door's own satisfied customers tell the story:

Excellent Quality

"Unlike other kettlebells I have used, Dragon Door is of far superior quality. You name it, Dragon Door has got it! Where other bells lack, Dragon Door kettlebells easily meet, if not exceed, what a bell is supposed to have in quality! Great balance, nice thick handle for grip strength, and a finish that won't destroy your hands when doing kettlebell exercises."
—Barry Adamson, Frederick, MD

New Dragon Door Bells— Best Ever!

"Just received a new e-coat 16 yesterday. Perfect balance, perfect texturing, non-slip paint, and absolutely seamless."
—Daniel Fazzari, Carson City, NV

Continually Impressed

"Dragon Door never fails to impress with their quality service and products. I bought the 16kg last month and since adding it to my kettlebell 'arsenal', I am seeing huge improvement from the heavier weight. I have larger hands for a woman so the handle on the 16kg fits my hands perfectly and it feels great...This is my fifth month using kettlebells and I cannot imagine NOT using them. They have changed my life." —Tracy Ann Mangold, Combined Locks, WI

Dragon Door bells just feel better

"I purchased this 35lb bell for a friend, and as I was carrying it to him I was thinking of ways I could keep it for myself. Everything about this bell is superior to other brands. The finish is the perfect balance of smooth and rough. The handle is ample in both girth and width even for a 35 lb bell, and the shape/ dimensions make overhead work so much more comfortable. There is a clear and noticeable difference between Dragon Door bells and others. Now I am looking to replace my cheap bells with Dragon Door's. On a related note, my friend is thrilled with his bell."—Raphael Sydnor, Woodberry Forest, VA

Made for Heavy-Duty Use!

"These kettlebells are definitely made for heavy-duty use! They are heftier than they appear, and the centrifugal force generated while swinging single or two-handed requires correct form. I have read numerous online reviews of different companies who manufacture kettlebells, and it I have yet to read a negative review of the kettlebells sold by Dragon Door. I have both the 35 and 44 lbs KBs, and I expect to receive a 53 lbs KB from Dragon Door by next week. And as I gain in strength and proficiency, I will likely order the 72 lbs KB. If you like to be challenged physically and enjoy pushing yourself, then buy a Russian Kettlebell and start swinging!"
—Mike Davis, Newman, CA

Dragon Door Kettlebells: The Real Deal!

"The differences between Dragon Door's authentic Russian kettlebell and the inferior one which I had purchased earlier at a local big box sports store are astounding! The Dragon Door design and quality are clearly superior, and your kettlebell just 'feels' right in my hand. There is absolutely no comparison (and yes, I returned the substandard hunk of iron to the big box store for a credit as soon as I received your kettlebell). I look forward to purchasing a heavier kettlebell from dragondoor.com as soon as I master the 16kg weight!"—Stephen Williams, Arlington, VA

CALL NOW: 1-800-899-5111 OR VISIT: www.dragondoor.com

Whatever Your Athletic Challenge, Dragon Door Has the Perfect Kettlebell Size to Meet Your Demand!

Classic Russian Kettlebells—All Cast Iron/E-Coated

 Russian Kettlebell 10 lbs. #P10N $41.75 *Call for shipping costs*

 Russian Kettlebell 16kg (35 lbs.) #P10A $96.75 *Call for shipping costs*

 Russian Kettlebell 32kg (70 lbs.) #P10C $153.94 *Call for shipping costs*

 Russian Kettlebell 14 lbs. #P10P $54.95 *Call for shipping costs*

 Russian Kettlebell 18kg (40 lbs.) #P10W $102.75 *Call for shipping costs*

 Russian Kettlebell 36kg (79 lbs.) #P10Q $175.95 *Call for shipping costs*

 Russian Kettlebell 18 lbs. #P10M $65.95 *Call for shipping costs*

 Russian Kettlebell 20kg (44 lbs.) #P10H $107.75 *Call for shipping costs*

 Russian Kettlebell 40kg (88 lbs.) #P10F $197.65 *Call for shipping costs*

 Russian Kettlebell 10kg (22 lbs.) #P10T $71.45 *Call for shipping costs*

 Russian Kettlebell 22kg (48 lbs.) #P10X $112.75 *Call for shipping costs*

 Russian Kettlebell 44kg (97 lbs.) #P10R $241.95 *Call for shipping costs*

 Russian Kettlebell 12kg (26 lbs.) #P10G $76.95 *Call for shipping costs*

 Russian Kettlebell 24kg (53 lbs.) #P10B $118.75 *Call for shipping costs*

 Russian Kettlebell 48kg (106 lbs.) #P10L $263.95 *Call for shipping costs*

 Russian Kettlebell 14kg (31 lbs.) #P10U $87.95 *Call for shipping costs*

 Russian Kettlebell 28kg (62 lbs.) #P10J $142.95 *Call for shipping costs*

· KETTLEBELLS ARE SHIPPED VIA UPS GROUND SERVICE, UNLESS OTHERWISE REQUESTED.

· KETTLEBELLS RANGING IN SIZE FROM 10 LBS. TO 24 KG CAN BE SHIPPED TO P.O. BOXES OR MILITARY ADDDRESSES VIA THE U.S. POSTAL SERVICE, BUT WE REQUIRE PHYSICAL ADDDRESSES FOR UPS DELIVERIES FOR ALL SIZES 32KG AND HEAVIER.

ALASKA/HAWAII KETTLEBELL ORDERING
Dragon Door now ships to all 50 states, including Alaska and Hawaii, via UPS Ground. 32kg and above available for RUSH (2-day air) shipment only.

CANADIAN KETTLEBELL ORDERING
Dragon Door now accepts online, phone and mail orders for Kettlebells to Canada, using UPS Standard service. UPS Standard to Canada service is guaranteed, fully tracked ground delivery, available to every address in all of Canada's 10 provinces. Delivery time can vary between 3 to 10 business days.

IMPORTANT — International shipping quotes & orders do not include customs clearance, duties, taxes or other non-routine customs brokerage charges, which are the responsibility of the customer.

CALL NOW: 1-800-899-5111 OR VISIT: www.dragondoor.com

1·800·899·5111
24 HOURS A DAY • FAX YOUR ORDER (866) 280-7619
ORDERING INFORMATION

Telephone Orders For faster service you may place your orders by calling Toll Free 24 hours a day, 7 days a week, 365 days per year. When you call, please have your credit card ready.

Customer Service Questions? Please call us between 9:00am– 11:00pm EST

Monday to Friday at 1-800-899-5111. Local and foreign customers call 513-346-4160 for orders and customer service

100% One-Year Risk-Free Guarantee. If you are not completely satisfied with any product—we'll be happy to give you a prompt exchange,

credit, or refund, as you wish. Simply return your purchase to us, and please let us know why you were dissatisfied—it will help us to provide better products and services in the future. *Shipping and handling fees are non-refundable.*

Complete and mail with full payment to: Dragon Door Publications, 5 County Road B East, Suite 3, Little Canada, MN 55117

Please print clearly
Sold To: A
Name_____

Street_____

City_____

State _____ Zip _____

Day phone*_____
* Important for clarifying questions on orders

Please print clearly
SHIP TO: *(Street address for delivery)*   B
Name_____

Street_____

City_____

State _____ Zip _____

Email_____

Warning to foreign customers:
The Customs in your country may or may not tax or otherwise charge you an additional fee for goods you receive. Dragon Door Publications is charging you only for U.S. handling and international shipping. Dragon Door Publications is in no way responsible for any additional fees levied by Customs, the carrier or any other entity.

ITEM #	QTY.	ITEM DESCRIPTION	ITEM PRICE	A OR B	TOTAL

HANDLING AND SHIPPING CHARGES • NO COD'S
Total Amount of Order Add (Excludes kettlebells and kettlebell kits):

$00.00 to 29.99	Add $6.00	$100.00 to 129.99	Add $14.00
$30.00 to 49.99	Add $7.00	$130.00 to 169.99	Add $16.00
$50.00 to 69.99	Add $8.00	$170.00 to 199.99	Add $18.00
$70.00 to 99.99	Add $11.00	$200.00 to 299.99	Add $20.00
		$300.00 and up	Add $24.00

Canada and Mexico add $6.00 to US charges. All other countries, flat rate, double US Charges. See Kettlebell section for Kettlebell Shipping and handling charges.

Total of Goods	
Shipping Charges	
Rush Charges	
Kettlebell Shipping Charges	
OH residents add 6.5% sales tax	
MN residents add 6.5% sales tax	
TOTAL ENCLOSED	

METHOD OF PAYMENT ❑ CHECK ❑ M.O. ❑ MASTERCARD ❑ VISA ❑ DISCOVER ❑ AMEX

Account No. *(Please indicate all the numbers on your credit card)*   EXPIRATION DATE

▢▢▢▢ ▢▢▢▢ ▢▢▢▢ ▢▢▢▢   ▢▢/▢▢

Day Phone: (___)_____

Signature: _____ **Date:** _____

NOTE: *We ship best method available for your delivery address. Foreign orders are sent by air. Credit card or International M.O. only. For **RUSH** processing of your order, add an additional $10.00 per address. Available on money order & charge card orders only.*

Errors and omissions excepted. Prices subject to change without notice.

1·800·899·5111

24 HOURS A DAY • FAX YOUR ORDER (866) 280-7619

O R D E R I N G   I N F O R M A T I O N

Telephone Orders For faster service you may place your orders by calling Toll Free 24 hours a day, 7 days a week, 365 days per year. When you call, please have your credit card ready.

Customer Service Questions? Please call us between 9:00am– 11:00pm EST

Monday to Friday at 1-800-899-5111. Local and foreign customers call 513-346-4160 for orders and customer service

100% One-Year Risk-Free Guarantee. If you are not completely satisfied with any product—we'll be happy to give you a prompt exchange,

credit, or refund, as you wish. Simply return your purchase to us, and please let us know why you were dissatisfied—it will help us to provide better products and services in the future. *Shipping and handling fees are non-refundable.*

Complete and mail with full payment to: Dragon Door Publications, 5 County Road B East, Suite 3, Little Canada, MN 55117

Please print clearly

Sold To: **A**

Name_____

Street_____

City_____

State_____ Zip _____

Day phone*_____
* Important for clarifying questions on orders

Please print clearly

SHIP TO: *(Street address for delivery)*   **B**

Name_____

Street_____

City_____

State_____ Zip _____

Email_____

Warning to foreign customers:
The Customs in your country may or may not tax or otherwise charge you an additional fee for goods you receive. Dragon Door Publications is charging you only for U.S. handling and international shipping. Dragon Door Publications is in no way responsible for any additional fees levied by Customs, the carrier or any other entity.

ITEM #	QTY.	ITEM DESCRIPTION	ITEM PRICE	A OR B	TOTAL

HANDLING AND SHIPPING CHARGES • NO COD'S
Total Amount of Order Add (Excludes kettlebells and kettlebell kits):

$00.00 to 29.99	Add $6.00	$100.00 to 129.99	Add $14.00
$30.00 to 49.99	Add $7.00	$130.00 to 169.99	Add $16.00
$50.00 to 69.99	Add $8.00	$170.00 to 199.99	Add $18.00
$70.00 to 99.99	Add $11.00	$200.00 to 299.99	Add $20.00
		$300.00 and up	Add $24.00

Canada and Mexico add $6.00 to US charges. All other countries, flat rate, double US Charges. See Kettlebell section for Kettlebell Shipping and handling charges.

Total of Goods	
Shipping Charges	
Rush Charges	
Kettlebell Shipping Charges	
OH residents add 6.5% sales tax	
MN residents add 6.5% sales tax	
TOTAL ENCLOSED	

METHOD OF PAYMENT ❏ CHECK ❏ M.O. ❏ MASTERCARD ❏ VISA ❏ DISCOVER ❏ AMEX

Account No. *(Please indicate all the numbers on your credit card)*   EXPIRATION DATE

□□□□ □□□□ □□□□ □□□□   □□/□□

Day Phone: (____)_____

Signature: _____   **Date:** _____

NOTE: *We ship best method available for your delivery address. Foreign orders are sent by air. Credit card or International M.O. only. For* **RUSH** *processing of your order, add an additional $10.00 per address. Available on money order & charge card orders only.*

Errors and omissions excepted. Prices subject to change without notice.

1·800·899·5111
24 HOURS A DAY • FAX YOUR ORDER (866) 280-7619
O R D E R I N G   I N F O R M A T I O N

Telephone Orders For faster service you may place your orders by calling Toll Free 24 hours a day, 7 days a week, 365 days per year. When you call, please have your credit card ready.

Customer Service Questions? Please call us between 9:00am– 11:00pm EST

Monday to Friday at 1-800-899-5111. Local and foreign customers call 513-346-4160 for orders and customer service

100% One-Year Risk-Free Guarantee. If you are not completely satisfied with any product—we'll be happy to give you a prompt exchange,

credit, or refund, as you wish. Simply return your purchase to us, and please let us know why you were dissatisfied—it will help us to provide better products and services in the future. *Shipping and handling fees are non-refundable.*

Complete and mail with full payment to: Dragon Door Publications, 5 County Road B East, Suite 3, Little Canada, MN 55117

Please print clearly
Sold To: A
Name_____
Street_____
City_____
State _____ Zip _____
Day phone*_____
* Important for clarifying questions on orders

Please print clearly
SHIP TO: *(Street address for delivery)*   B
Name_____
Street_____
City_____
State _____ Zip _____
Email_____

Warning to foreign customers:
The Customs in your country may or may not tax or otherwise charge you an additional fee for goods you receive. Dragon Door Publications is charging you only for U.S. handling and international shipping. Dragon Door Publications is in no way responsible for any additional fees levied by Customs, the carrier or any other entity.

ITEM #	QTY.	ITEM DESCRIPTION	ITEM PRICE	A OR B	TOTAL

HANDLING AND SHIPPING CHARGES • NO COD'S
Total Amount of Order Add (Excludes kettlebells and kettlebell kits):

$00.00 to 29.99	Add $6.00	$100.00 to 129.99	Add $14.00
$30.00 to 49.99	Add $7.00	$130.00 to 169.99	Add $16.00
$50.00 to 69.99	Add $8.00	$170.00 to 199.99	Add $18.00
$70.00 to 99.99	Add $11.00	$200.00 to 299.99	Add $20.00
		$300.00 and up	Add $24.00

Canada and Mexico add $6.00 to US charges. All other countries, flat rate, double US Charges. See Kettlebell section for Kettlebell Shipping and handling charges.

Total of Goods	
Shipping Charges	
Rush Charges	
Kettlebell Shipping Charges	
OH residents add 6.5% sales tax	
MN residents add 6.5% sales tax	
TOTAL ENCLOSED	

METHOD OF PAYMENT ❑ CHECK ❑ M.O. ❑ MASTERCARD ❑ VISA ❑ DISCOVER ❑ AMEX

Account No. *(Please indicate all the numbers on your credit card)*   EXPIRATION DATE

☐☐☐☐ ☐☐☐☐ ☐☐☐☐ ☐☐☐☐   ☐☐/☐☐

Day Phone: (____)_____

Signature: _____   Date: _____

NOTE: *We ship best method available for your delivery address. Foreign orders are sent by air. Credit card or International M.O. only. For* **RUSH** *processing of your order, add an additional $10.00 per address. Available on money order & charge card orders only.*

Errors and omissions excepted. Prices subject to change without notice.

1·800·899·5111

24 HOURS A DAY • FAX YOUR ORDER (866) 280-7619

O R D E R I N G   I N F O R M A T I O N

Telephone Orders For faster service you may place your orders by calling Toll Free 24 hours a day, 7 days a week, 365 days per year. When you call, please have your credit card ready.

Customer Service Questions? Please call us between 9:00am– 11:00pm EST

Monday to Friday at 1-800-899-5111. Local and foreign customers call 513-346-4160 for orders and customer service

100% One-Year Risk-Free Guarantee. If you are not completely satisfied with any product—we'll be happy to give you a prompt exchange,

credit, or refund, as you wish. Simply return your purchase to us, and please let us know why you were dissatisfied—it will help us to provide better products and services in the future. *Shipping and handling fees are non-refundable.*

Complete and mail with full payment to: Dragon Door Publications, 5 County Road B East, Suite 3, Little Canada, MN 55117

Please print clearly

Sold To: **A**

Name_____

Street _____

City _____

State _____ Zip _____

Day phone*_____
* Important for clarifying questions on orders

Please print clearly

SHIP TO: *(Street address for delivery)* **B**

Name_____

Street _____

City _____

State _____ Zip _____

Email _____

Warning to foreign customers:
The Customs in your country may or may not tax or otherwise charge you an additional fee for goods you receive. Dragon Door Publications is charging you only for U.S. handling and international shipping. Dragon Door Publications is in no way responsible for any additional fees levied by Customs, the carrier or any other entity.

ITEM #	QTY.	ITEM DESCRIPTION	ITEM PRICE	A OR B	TOTAL

HANDLING AND SHIPPING CHARGES • NO COD'S
Total Amount of Order Add (Excludes kettlebells and kettlebell kits):

$00.00 to 29.99	Add $6.00	$100.00 to 129.99	Add $14.00
$30.00 to 49.99	Add $7.00	$130.00 to 169.99	Add $16.00
$50.00 to 69.99	Add $8.00	$170.00 to 199.99	Add $18.00
$70.00 to 99.99	Add $11.00	$200.00 to 299.99	Add $20.00
		$300.00 and up	Add $24.00

Canada and Mexico add $6.00 to US charges. All other countries, flat rate, double US Charges. See Kettlebell section for Kettlebell Shipping and handling charges.

Total of Goods	
Shipping Charges	
Rush Charges	
Kettlebell Shipping Charges	
OH residents add 6.5% sales tax	
MN residents add 6.5% sales tax	
TOTAL ENCLOSED	

METHOD OF PAYMENT ❏ CHECK ❏ M.O. ❏ MASTERCARD ❏ VISA ❏ DISCOVER ❏ AMEX

Account No. *(Please indicate all the numbers on your credit card)*   EXPIRATION DATE

☐☐☐☐ ☐☐☐☐ ☐☐☐☐ ☐☐☐☐   ☐☐/☐☐

Day Phone: (___)_____

Signature: _____   **Date:** _____

NOTE: *We ship best method available for your delivery address. Foreign orders are sent by air. Credit card or International M.O. only. For **RUSH** processing of your order, add an additional $10.00 per address. Available on money order & charge card orders only.*

Errors and omissions excepted. Prices subject to change without notice.